Ra'mi Tiye Sekhmet

Presents

"The Veil"

A novel based on an
African American tragedy
that turns into triumph...

Copyright: 2016 by the Original Publisher

ISBN: - 13 978-1541259980

10 – 154125998X

Printed in the U.S.A.
Original Self publisher
Ra'mi Tiye Sekhmet

Amazon.com

Table of Contents

Dedication

Addendum

Introduction

Novel

Authors Page

Dedication

The written material is a large spiritual portal as I envisioned it based briefly on a revelation that my ancestors made known to me. Throughout, imaginary and distinguished dreams which was a sacred intimate communion that I experienced with a divine beloved being. During this encounter I was somewhat lifted and elevated into a higher and deeply rooted dimension. Somehow, the passage into this distinct place was an unaccustomed and unexpected burst of splendor. It was within a small portion of a heavenly access into an angelic space of empowerment. Therefore, I believe that I was to undergo some sort of observation concerning a solar system characteristic in a distant far away sphere. Overall, to transform myself and connect into this space of a sovereign power and newfound existence. However, as I completely relied on this mind blowing awakening and unexpected glorious spirit filled throne. Likewise, it is of my best interest to bestow and share this fantastic and remarkable journey concerning the heritage of aboriginal people. In this story I felt compelled to reserve the work and dedicated it on behalf of the betterment of my people. The indigenous black brothers and sisters on this beautiful planet earth (ship) with the hope of returning them to their former glory and status in the world. Although, my people have endured tremendous struggles due to enslavement and the concealment of their roots. I plan to exonerate my findings and not except a needless impression of my literary composition. Otherwise, in doing so, address concerns that advocate a higher degree of knowledge, containing ancient African occult wisdom. Primarily, in spite of appreciating efforts that were made by others who intended to help solve our problems and dilemmas on behalf of brothers and sisters. Instead, many formed decisions based on misconceptions, ignorance and suspicions concerning the smallest little details. Trying to exalt and vindicate short comings in a plot to hinder improvement within the culture by intending to formulate a greater understanding for themselves. Overall, throughout my adversity this book is written in defense of the righteous, it's my hope to enrich peace, connect with the spirit of ancestors, knowledge, prosperity and healing for those who deserve it. Equally, choose to improve our present circumstance by embracing each other on one accord as we move towards restoring our souls with happy loving moments into our lives once again.

Addendum

An enormous sequence of events took place that tried to prevent this written composition from completing and launching into the book arena. It was an exhausting literary project that required much attention but, I was determined to finish the process to finalize my work. However, I was under a stupendous attack by my own people of African descent who aggressively criticized my level of consciousness. Before realizing that this book was a prophesized prediction since my youth which may cause change for the betterment of my people and citizens as a whole. Although, I rebelled against putting together the material until the year 2014 when the root of my family tree ascended into a constellation of stars. The ruling class of black supreme authority when I began to gather divine knowledge that was already inside of me. As I struggled to finish the text brothers and sisters began to feel compelled to challenge my theory concerning the people of antiquity. Overall, the work was based on a considerable amount of research that I undertook to balance out what was made known to me naturally. Substantially, after allowing others to glimpse at the book cover in order to raise funds to publish the book. Acquaintances assumed that they were affiliated with my recordings and tried to belittle my efforts with their own philosophy whereas, they're emphasis on the subject accelerated. However, I was approached with comments by my people who apparently possessed a small level of African study. Predominantly, someone would think that these individuals were a scholar who dominate an advanced degree of Knowledge after giving they're opinion on the topic. At the time I didn't realize that the book cover would impact mobs of brothers and sisters who I noticed quoting proverbs from passages. The impression that I received after quotes were stolen from my writings during lots moments of stalking me led to an endless solitude of privacy. However, the aura that I received from strangers were so, profound that the reality of a successful novel became inevitable as the photo inspired many to become writers. I had no private study to develop the literature so, I had to rely on social institutions to complete the book. People then insisted on proving a different analysis to claim what was mine when the opportunity presented itself by applying their own wisdom and sell it. Somehow, these people seemed confused concerning their own awareness after critiquing my unreleased writings by limiting an evaluation of my work. The novel is based on spirituality which may not exonerate religious and political concepts or groups. However, I don't contemplate to infringe on anyone which is not my inquiry of biblical scripture neither otherwise. Principally, it's my theory that convey parallel versions of creation verses the metaphysical aspect of the primordial universe. Therefore, I believe that it's every individual responsibility to decipher what has been giving to them by taking time to seek the truth and decide what is real verses an illusion. Although, this novel was written for entertainment and not to take too an excessive degree of regret or anger.

Ra'mi Tiye Sekhmet

presents

"The Veil"

A novel based on an
African American tragedy
which turns into triumph...

Introduction

During the 21st century in America at the beginning of spring a very distinct birth takes place of a special female child. The new born was placed into a masterful made hand weaved cradle accenting precious stones, crystals and cowrie shells. In the unique designed baby's bed she laid within a multi-colored swaddling cloth. Made with love for wrapping the infant as a gift from grandma who is a descendant of west Africa. The child is an ancestor compassed of the early dynastic period conveying the indigenous people from a sacred royal lineage. A reincarnated primordial egg traveling through the universe which is governed from a majestic lodging which claim the embryo. The geographical location of the throne is designated in regards to the golden tree of life from the cosmos and landed on earth. However, the child delivered into this world with a veil over her face by the hands of a mid-wife in a friendly black community setting. A family of nine who's skin tone is ebony with wooly hair and live in a simply designed red brick home overlooking a decorative landscape which is well maintained. The infant's mother and grandmother are a poor working underclass in the healthcare profession in Brooklyn, New York. The child is a divine being in tune with the universe and her complexion was the color of earth bronze, in nature and blessed by the Sun. The infant bestows a unique quality in her own persona and enormous vessel that is of splendor and full of grace. However, during mother's pregnancy the baby was always calm and gentle not like her siblings who were restless possessing rebellious souls. Overall, mom had a healthy child and named her Gen short for Genesis because of her wonderful and amazing birth. Anyway, mother was frightened by the diamond shaped membrane which was over the infants face until grandmother explained that the veil is an ancient Kemet prophecy. Someday, Genesis will grow up to be the deliverer of her people freeing them from a system of oppression and become a great morally acclaimed citizen. The veil symbolizes celestial and notorious power out of the universal which is inspired through a divine bloodline. Genesis will have a strong connection with her ancestors and a great spiritual purpose on earth for the better of man. Mother then becomes envious of the ancient Kemet prophecy foretold by grandma and seek to rob her child of her blessing by stealing the powers. Mother don't believe in spirituality but, rather a gloomy world of fear as she practiced witchcraft day and night to steal the gift. When Genesis becomes an adult she met a female African spiritualist (witch) who revealed the special birth and enlightens her on to how to activate the energy. The devotional woman explained to Genesis that energy can manifest into greatness and create 360 degrees of power out of the universe. Therefore, at the appointed season natural components will release into the circuits of her body. Importantly, creating a black goddess who orbits throughout outer space from a gravitational current naturally pulling her on a flying winged disk (Heru Behudet) in a close encounter with the stars (family). Leading Genesis into a battle of retribution against the enslavers of a dominating and evil empire on earth. Although, the task would be difficult for Genesis she wasn't resilient to change neither lazy or rebellious and couldn't fail because the ancestors were with her. Later, Genesis began to perform miraculous and unusual task leaving the public totally spellbound where acquaintances seek to find the source of her power. Overall, Genesis ancestors demanded that she liberate and train brothers and sisters for a mighty uprising against the system who were responsible for organizing violent crimes against innocent people. Afterwards, the dreadful war ended in a stock pile of corpse caused the wicked empire to fall as the landmass realigned for change. Now, the village then celebrated the return to the homeland from out of the hell that they suffered and finally was happy after a long miserable journey. Then the Sun (Ra) chose to reclaim essence again as the earth was cleansed and renewed for the children of the universal creator. The village began chanting sweet songs of freedom and celebrating by fragrant the air with aromas of frankincense, myrrh and sandalwood. Drummers were drumming, potters are potting, weavers were weaving and beading jewelry as brothers and sisters embraced and one another. Then the children on the earth rejoiced and they occupied the land with loving happy moments long and festive. Therefore, the ancient Kemet prophecy of the veil came true by taking the young woman on an incredible and spiral journey that no longer led to confusion. However, Genesis never lost sight of her faith but, nothing could have prepared her for the coming dilemma, loss, miseducation, lies, and trickery to get to her purpose.

Destiny!

My name is Ra'mi Tiye Sekhmet who is a sister of African descent which had an enlightened and breathtaking experience on my journey throughout this life. Therefore, the spirit led me to write an ultimate and compelling story to instruct you for betterment by making it known in sharing an awakening encounter concerning the aboriginal people of those individuals who will appreciate my efforts.

"The Veil"

Chapter 1

The Birth of a deliverer

This story is based on some true events. It is the 21st century in America and the beginning of spring when a distinct birth takes place under Orion's belt and the brightest star. The fertilized egg developed into many cells which created a blessed female child in the countryside of New York. The genealogy of a supernatural plan specially aligned in the constellation of luminary bodies appearing as a fixed point of light bringing about creation from immortal to mortal. The connection of the birth of man came from the stars to begin a civilization out of an abomination from a rooted cosmic tree. The transition to earth was for rehabilitation and is on a lower frequency but, is where the opportunity to restore the soul can be granted. The infant was born with a veil over her face and placed into a masterful made hand weaved cradle accenting precious crystals and stones. Amethyst representing spirituality, quartz for clarity, topaz for healing and cowrie shells symbolizing wealth. In the unique designed bed laid the baby wrapped within a multi-colored swaddling cloth. Made with love for wrapping the infant as a gift from grandma who is a pleasant descendant from west Africa. The infant's bloodline is from the indigenous people within a sacred royal lineage out of Kemet. A blessed reincarnated super embryo that is governed from a majestic lodging regarding the golden tree of life. The baby is in tune with the universe and magnificent glories as her complexion is the color of earth bronze in nature when kissed by the nurturing Sun (Ra). The youngster Bestow a unique quality in her own persona and enormous vessel that is full of splendor and grace. Delivered into the world by the hands of a mid-wife under the protection of her grandma who refused to allow DNA tampering. The delivery of the child took place in a low-income black community built on a brown stone foundation overlooking a decorative landscape and well maintained. As the child comes of age grandma buried the crystals and cowrie shells into the earth during a full moon for accessing life force energies. The whole family was ebony and the household interior had no metaphysical items, tapestries, artifacts, journals, essential oil but, a small library of literature that grandma owned. The infant wasn't born of privilege because of mother and grandmother worked in an underclass healthcare background. Although, the baby was happy, blessed with an amazing spiritual and spectacular aura born 5th of 6 siblings. Mother was attractive with kinky hair and a short chunky bodily profile focusing on English in high school and love to travel. During mother's pregnancy the special child was always calm and gentle not like her brothers and sister, restless with rebellious souls. Therefore, the child was named Gen short for Genesis because of her special and profound birth. Mother didn't experience a covering over the face of her other children and was frightened concerning the membrane thinking something was wrong with the baby. Now, grandma didn't have much education but, she had common sense, full of wisdom, strong, stern in her thinking, short, spunky, heavy set and fun loving. Grandma consumed liquor heavily and on a regular basis and explained the meaning to her daughter that the veil is an old ancient Kemet prophecy. A sacred mystery system of rare births which are a part of the primordial egg meaning the coming of another world that is pure. Therefore, Genesis is destined to appear in heaven as well as on earth having a clairvoyant soul encouraging correctness to those who are open minded towards the change. The child must not mix her race for the reason in west Africa it was prohibited and the indigenous ones were warned not to follow other groups who engaged in different practices that will end in disaster. However, the prophecy entails a coming deliverer who will fight against the injustice of the people who are oppressed within a dominating and evil empire. Therefore, Genesis is the sacrificial lamb (savior) who will suffer to awake and lead her people out of bondage. Genesis bloodline comes from a kingly threshold and is favored by an ancient monarch but, her veil refers to the protection she sustains while guiding her people to understand themselves. Genesis blessings are in the range of leadership, healing and greater insight when her ancestors speak to her through dreams and visions (revelations). Genesis was born with this calling pushing her destiny into a reality that beholds greatness as many enemies will make it their mission to eliminate her. The assailant agenda will fail miserably because the descendants are with her as the purpose forge. The ancestors knew that they could trust Genesis to carry the burden of this generation and sacrifice her own happiness in order to fulfill the will of the Most High. Meanwhile, Genesis wasn't taught to support black functions, movements and businesses or not even a black owned newspaper although she knew that it was the right thing to do. After grandma revealed the African folklore to her daughter she then mentioned that there is more than one creation story. You have the Kemet creation story where in the beginning there is Nun the dark waters of chaos. One day a hill rose up out of the waters called Ben-Ben and on the hill stood Atum the first god. Atum coughed and spat out (soul) Shu god of the air and Tefnut goddess of moisture. Shu and Tefnut had two children, Geb the god of the earth and Nut the goddess of the sky. Shu lifted up Nut so that she became a canopy over Geb then Nut and Geb had four children Asuar, Aset, Seth and Nephthys. Asuar was a righteous King and the ruler over the earth and Aset his African queen of the royal house. Sut became Seth (lower self) and pale when he was jealous of Asuar because he wanted to be the ruler on earth. One day he killed Asuar and he went down into the underworld then Seth remained to rule as king on earth. Asuar and Aset had one son called Heru who battled against Seth and regained the throne as the ruling king on earth and Asuar was the king of the underworld (judgement). Now, my daughter grandma said you also have a Sumerian creation story of a mixed breed goddess Nammu evolving out of the primordial sea giving birth to Anki the universe god (heaven and earth). Anki produced a son Enil the air god and out of that creation comes the moon goddess Nanna and the sun god Utu. Later, in the heavens during a drunken banquet the gods decided to create humans and descended them to earth. Afterwards, humans had many problems surviving because they refuse to give credit to their creators so, the gods decide to destroy them. Now, this Hindu creation story is more reduced than the others there is no heaven. A dark ocean washed upon the shores licking the edges of night and a large cobra showed up on the sea within its endless coils laying Vishnu to be watched over by the serpent. During silence and peace Vishnu slept from a dream then came the depths of a humming sound that started a trembled ohm growing spreading empty energy. As the night ended Vishnu awoke by dawn and from the navel grew a lovely lotus flower within the middle of the blossom. There sat Vishnu's servant Brahma awaiting the lords command while speaking to his servant it's time to begin creation so Brahma vowed Vishnu's motion. A wind swept the waters then Vishnu and the serpent vanished and Brahma remained in the lotus flower floating on the sea. He lifted up his arms calming the wind and ocean then brahma split the lotus flower into three stretching one part into earth with a 3rd part of the flower he created the sky. On the earth he created the grass, flowers, trees, various plants, animals and insects to live on the land. He made many birds and fish giving all creatures a sense of smell, touch by giving them power to see, hear and move now the world is filled with life. Grandma told her daughter another Christianity creation story that is based on the worship of Serapis and the council of Nicea. This assembly created a false image of Jesus Christ who most people believe today is a pale family who father is named Jehovah. The parents are Mary and Joseph and they're son has a recessive gene and is from the origin of scorching Africa. This was when hieroglyphics wasn't written in English until around the 1600's when black people were slaves and English names was forced on them. Later, Jesus is educated in Egypt during his return to Jerusalem the local priest was angry about his mysterious teaching. However, they started spreading malicious gossip leading up to his death then he was crucified by the orders of Pontius Pilate and rose on the 3rd day. Afterwards, grandma discuss these stories with her daughter conveying that every race has their own cultural differences. Then she continued to mention that the ancestors are pleased with Genesis and she will grow up to be a morally acclaimed citizen. The veil symbolizes her celestial, notorious power and in the appointed season Genesis will become a universal goddess who elevated out of a divine bloodline. She will have a strong connection with her ancestors and given a spiritual purpose on earth when the church (fraud) is replaced by the celestial tree and the spell of Kingu is broken. The sacred domain in the heavens is much more advanced than earth and has existed much longer than this civilization, pure, rich and full of natural resources. However, Genesis will release energy activated by universal substances causing her to become ageless as her body begins to transform into a new soul. Then a dramatic climate change will shortly take place on the earth surface resulting into major pieces of mass realigning. Then the shift will re-attach to the African continent reclaiming the land and a spiritual standard of living. Grandma had consumed a lot of alcoholic beverages by this time so, she continued to tell her daughter that in the beginning of creation people of African descent were free. They lived during the sun cycle and was the only beings in existence until a race of hybrids were created out of the germ of original man (lower part). The deities were harmonious with nature and the wonderful attributes but, one of them went against the master plan. Then produced a species that wouldn't reason with the innovative way of living and took it upon themselves to alter society for material gain (third dimension). The indigenous people were the witnesses of the most high's creation but, chose to worship false gods that caused them to fall onto a lower frequency becoming a mortal soul and no longer gods. These acts angered the universal creator and allowed the gigantic continental divide to drift separating humanity resulting in an ungodly habitat (hell). Although, the children of the all mighty will have the opportunity to restore their soul after warriors are sent to help correct the imperfections. Therefore, the African warriors will be sent to break the spell of Kingu and bring the truth to their people and ready them to go back to the roots. The heritage of the aboriginal people, is a tradition handed down from the past and they can't return to the family tree without the knowledge of it. Therefore, our people lost their freedom when this corrupt species was created by a kinship of the all mighty god. That family member had knowledge of science and rebelled against the original plan causing a battle of good against evil. After the deities fell from grace and became an abomination they taught the new beings sacred African occult wisdom concerning the life of antiquity. Whereas, out of original man's stupidity the salvage beast stored various animals in warehouses confined in crowded cages and pens individually stalled to mutate the indigenous ones into mankind and will be no longer pure. Therefore, the new species who were created could only exist on the third dimension (earth) because of lack of pigment and the second dimension would be many of those people permanent home (hell). These new creatures discovered through a science experiment of genetic testing that a breed who can't produce carbon (color) is not excepted by nature and neither can they formulate a color substance. This concept angered the modern species so, they continued to change the frequency (balance) of the aboriginal people's nature for control. Then the proto-type of the universal creator may not return to their former glory and settle for false images of god creating their own set of rules. After modifying humanity into salvage beast for advocates of evil they continued on a dominating and corrupt path by eliminating good and rewarding evil on the planet. Therefore, the all mighty creator proclaimed that it is a curse to breed outside of the race because carbonites are not from the same place and will not enter the same place. The results of rebelling against all mighty god would cause a fall into a lower dimension where there is no opportunity to restore the soul. In grandma's determination to expose the truth she told her daughter that when you make yourself available to an enemy who aren't capable of righteousness because of a calcification (cruel) you will never get justice. A recessive gene has a totally different DNA make-up which can't be reproduced without carbon (color) and a dominant gene can't function properly off of a network of a discrepancy of energy. This recessive species can't survive in winter when organisms can't reproduce (grow) and cells die but, they even run air conditioning during cold seasons. After a scientific development of the recessive gene proved a totally different reality than colored subjects. Perpetually, meaning these kind of people are the lower part of you but, later mother will become weak and choose to honor the misconception. Many generations have passed while the indigenous people have suffered at the hands of corrupt rulers who were obviously playing out an illusion of existing and ungodly. However, until the sons and daughters of the all mighty god prove themselves worthy and honorable they will remain denied of returning to their former glory and natural way of life. The spirit of the recessive breed can't ascend without carbon but, shall continue to remain in 3D until the timeline of this creation expires. Genesis will soon come of age and she is going to answer the call from the ancestors to bring change on the planet and she will then meet her descendant that live in that great big skyline. Meanwhile, a great battle of retribution against good people who possess a peaceful and loving nature will end in resistance. Then Genesis will break every chain of oppression that her people had to endure on earth and return them to freedom. Genesis will encounter cosmic activity cultivating in the atmosphere absorbing throughout her body creating a new being by causing the circuits in her body to transform into incredible strength during an adrenaline rush. Also, as carbon is more frequently produced in higher concentrations of color expressing blackness converting Genesis thinking into a lucid genius while her body has become a wall of armor. Someday, she will learn how to manifest the seven deities (energy) within herself during a meditation session. The concept was inspired by Genesis kinsmen the Orisha's who are the seven deities. The spirit of theses deities Genesis will learn to call upon in times of trouble who represent all that is sacred and powerful. Then Genesis will develop the science of tapping into her pineal gland which will be the access to her ancestors through telepathic communication within the cosmic tree. Also, Genesis will possess other powers but, a special ability is manipulating objects as powerful as steel using her thick long locked hair. Hair induced of wool as the 9 Ether particle become a weapon of war... and it will be hell for anyone who will try to get in Genesis way. Otherwise, the pineal gland can open too! by cultivating sounds of echoing rhythms as she fast conserving a plant source diet allowing clairvoyant energy to access. Moreover, when the universe navigate itself into an original format then the goddess can manifest power for the day of retribution. However, Genesis will begin seeing objects that are strange to her which is necessary for her to open the pathway when guardians are ready to make contact. In grandma's enthusiasm she continued to drink heavy as she went on to inform her daughter about the chosen child that she gave birth to will never be a traitor for the emancipation of her people. Genesis will be a few of aboriginals who become conscious of who they are but, many who don't will be dangerous to themselves and others. However, the evil and malicious assailants will be in a desperate attempt to match Genesis power as the timeline to rule expires. Additionally, on this planet and they continue to deceive people into thinking that salvation is through religion but, they know that the deliverer is in the mist of the black community. Otherwise, when they attempt to locate the hero (Heru) they will use laboratories to experiment on elevating power by manipulating DNA samples. Meanwhile, the enemies of righteousness who searched for a completed analysis equivalent to Genesis will undertake an unsuccessful discovery of corrupting cells that can't match a species more superior. Likewise, they will fail miserably and their evil intentions will end in an unsettled catastrophe when it's revealed that nothing is more powerful than mother nature and god can manifest into everything that is in existence. Therefore, Genesis will be a great one and misunderstood by others as her gift of divine power will be a curse and challenging but, she will endure to get to her destiny. After grandma explained the ancient folklore that was overheard by siblings who noticed that Genesis was much different than they. Siblings couldn't except that she was self-sufficient, charming, talented with a perfect bodily form which caused jealousy and mischief among the family. Considering that the family were church going religious people who didn't miss a Sunday service which made it seem more ridiculous to envy Genesis. Later, Genesis experienced horrifying moments with these church members who can't be trusted using religion to hide their evil disposition to fool the people into thinking that religion is the solution to salvation. Now, mother has a high I.Q. so, grandma decided to invest money in her daughter's education by enrolling her into college. Out of mother's negligence and rebellion she loses her opportunity and try's to compensate the ruin by stealing Genesis blessing. Although, Genesis was born nearly 17 generations after the Atlantic slave trade when enemy ships titled Jesus were zooming to pursue their evil ambition against the indigenous people who were financed by a Spanish queen name Isabella. These people are descendants of a defiant seed who intentions were to betray the universal creator by replacing a divine purpose. Torturing Africans who were stolen from their homeland, separating them from their families and taken to America for the sole purpose of slave labor. When the children of all mighty god turned away from their creator and the results was they lost their protection from the supreme deities. Therefore, the adversary took advantage of the stupidity and took their tongue replacing vegetarian and vegan diets with the slaughtering of animals for food. It caused an astronomical record of ruined health as the Africans nutritional plant source diet became a thing of the past. After Africans were enslaved Caucasian's began to impersonate and learn from their knowledge while they concealed their culture, traditions and historical past which was they're gateway to the ancients. Meanwhile, African's chromosomes were used in laboratories for mutation by exchanging DNA samples from colored subjects to non-colored subjects. It was for the survival of hemophiliacs who disconnected the indigenous people form their divine source of supreme power. Otherwise, grandma told her daughter about the early 1600's when black slaves were bought to America and a committee of slave owners was formed to find out how to strip the people of antiquity from their power. Then a male house nigger named Henry who was threated physically by his slave owner, master Sanders who mentioned to his slave how talented the niggers were. Then master Sanders said to Henry if you refuse to tell the source of their power that he would be killed. Out of fear of master Sanders outburst Henry told the secret it is in their atoms and hair (9 ether). Radiate their environment and food, mix their genes, remove them from nature which is their true source of power and they will become completely useless then you will have full control over your slaves. Moreover, master Sanders smiled informing his wife Martha to proclaim an order all over the south that a process will begin the deactivation of power of African occult wisdom. Therefore, African history, traditions and culture was concealed within that generation of slaves and the offspring. Then a field nigger name Jessie heard the snitch from an open window and later threaten to kill Henry by chocking him to death for telling the secret of the African mystery system. Before the attack on Henry by Jessie slave owner Sanders had Henry hanged from a tree near a river. It's where the spirit spoke to slaves concerning their suffering and nearby slave owners enjoyed the lynching over a drunken feast. Slave masters understood the concept of Arab Islam (mixed breed) against African Islam (revolutionary) over the invasion of African territory on a race for capitalizing. However, Caucasians decided to create a theory of owning wealth and power by colonializing in the regions of the motherland. Then they continued repeatedly raping Africans for mix breeding, stealing their culture, rich natural resources, burning them alive, cannibalizing, butchering and hanging them, stripping them of their history and way of life. They separated Africans from their families until it brought about endless loving concepts of family seized to no longer exist. After removing Africans of their knowledge and conditioning them for failure slave owners continued to discover, explorer, conqueror and claim new territories. As the slave ships continued to enter the coastline of America called the new world to European settlers. During a long and deplorable journey of Africans stolen from the motherland forced to the new world for enslavement bound and chained naked, lying in unthinkable and nasty conditions. Although, the captivity resulted in over two million men, women and children deaths along the navigation. An awaiting group of Caucasians put blacks into forcible labor daily at gun point on southern plantations picking cotton, rice and tobacco crops without pay. Then mother comment on what grandma told her by saying I can't imagine surviving during those times. Grandma continued to say that the killings and martyring prolonged until generations after African slaves obtained their freedom. Therefore, every black network or movement that came into power who fought for freedom, justice and equality including scientist and teachers. Caucasian groups still refused to accept equal rights for all people until they realized that surviving without black people were impossible and used informers to benefit by selling out their people (brief Malcolm X speech plays). Medgar Evers, Stokley Carmicheal, Khalid Muhammad, Marcus Garvey, Harriet Tubman, Winnie Mandela, Nat Turner, Malcolm X, Patrice Lumumba, Stephen Biko, the Black Panther Party, Professor Delbert Blair, Doctor Sebi, Doctor Frances Cress Welsing to name a few black prophets, teachers and leaders. The acts against our prophets and messengers were so gruesome that it was nearly impossible to commensurate their legacy. In fear of Caucasians political authority black people gave up the fight against oppression and still today serving one slave master in exchange for the next believing that someone of

Caucasian descent will liberate the black class. Although, African Americans were victims of Caucasian terrorist since the Atlantic slave trade and still today while they are denied equal rights and refused reparations. In efforts to return these victims to their African roots and give them compensation for the removal of their languages and way of life as our brother Marcus Garvey planned in regards to his back to Africa legacy before he was murdered. In Africa our brother Steven Biko who was killed by the same beast fighting against the invasion of Caucasian rule in south Africa by robing the indigenous people of their land while suffering from apartheid. Also, Nelson Mandela who was an anti-apartheid activist which addressed a speech before his imprisonment stated that there was no need for non-violence negotiations with a group of people who are salvages. Therefore, grandma said beware in the 21st century when brothers and sisters are called buddy or friend it's just the enemies way to decipher if you are a house nigga or a field nigga to maintain power and control (set-up). Largely, we won't forget Alexander the great who led a bloody massacre against the people of antiquity replacing our African heritage with a false concept of religion that teaches brothers and sisters forgiveness while the slaughter continues. The aftermath of this salvage act played a misleading game by indoctrinating self-hate which caused division in the family and a lack of connecting with the higher self. However, the system pretended to care for African Americans welfare by influencing them to accept a program designed to solve to the problems. Additionally, a few brothers and sisters are barely keeping the African presence alive but, love, hug, kiss, fallow and participate in other groups celebrations. While they ignore their own culture and unbelievably mix-breed with offspring of the former slave owner thinking life will be better is a fool. Therefore, this war is against aboriginal people who have pigment which is found in the hair, skin, iris and initiated in most natural organisms. Those beings who are color deficient producing lighter skin tones are a 6 ether species which represent blonde hair and can get burned or skin cancer after spending only a few minutes in the sun (ra). However, color can act as a filter to prevent damage of a delicate layer of the skin and withstand sun exposure up to 1250 degrees of Fahrenheit and still retain properties. Therefore, European's was in a desperate need to learn Kemet Magic and knowledge from of our Yoruba spiritualist on how to use supernatural forces but, for demonic purposes to gain control. However, the beast is trying to win the war against the indigenous people and will end in defeat because of Ra the magnetic Sun god who activates power when reclaiming the planet. Therefore, many aboriginal people who are suffering from grief will try to ease their pain by attacking their own people thinking that they would be rewarded by the beast. Likewise, other groups across the globe have no respect for brothers and sisters who are placed in a position of authority and abuse it. Moreover, informers for the beast will become obsolete when they're not needed anymore because they would just be a constant reminder of what sustains life which they don't have, carbon the ultimate power. A recessive gene Grandma goes on to say wasn't created for eternal life but, to put the dominant gene through hell. The bloodline of a recessive gene can be traced from all dogs with various color of hair carrying the same trait of their ancestors. Meanwhile, during segregation when every race was divided achieving their own market place black people were more loving toward one another and maintained successful millionaire businesses. At that time Caucasians were falling economically losing control so they decided to emerge into the civil rights movement enforcing integration in order to position themselves to regain power. Deceiving aboriginal people into excepting low wage jobs which pushed them into extreme poverty. However, offering higher positons of employment to black people who degraded themselves by imitating an artificial image and work under substitute terms. Overall, the time had come to reverse the evil plan of the enemy greed then along came Genesis to reinforce it. In season the redeemer will arrive to free the enslaved children of the all mighty god and remove them from the bondage that they suffered at the hands of the ungodly. Genesis will have no clue that she is the one responsible for the freedom of her people until she is contacted by the ancestors. Since Genesis ancestors were from the stars a world far away in the cosmos where the structure is operated and navigated on natural substances in the universe. The Sun (Ra) and its brightness and the shimmering moon will be in the mist of Genesis twilight offering beautiful crystals, stones, colorful jewels, gold, and precious metals that comforts her. Additionally, platinum, uranium and other gifts such as oil which was plentiful on other civilizations where Genesis relatives live. Likewise, accentuating the atmosphere within its glory and decor while extending these heartwarming gifts in favor of Genesis. Meanwhile, Grandma also, told her daughter that change will come to America for betterment of the children of god and Genesis wouldn't be resistant to it, lazy or rebellious and her power will be extraordinary in battle. She is going to be used for a divine purpose and an uprising that leads to freedom and nothing or no one could stop the demand of the universal creator.

Chapter 2

The wicked mother

Mother watched Genesis with an intense degree of hatred while she was growing up keeping the secret about the special birth of her daughter to herself. Genesis is now a young teen who is electrifying with creative ideas and has a soulful demeanor as she up hold elegance. Her height is average and she is petite with a curly afro, extremely attractive, talented and intelligent just like her dad. Genesis father was a humble man that served in the army and she was his favorite among the siblings. A peaceful man with a strong since of humor, average height with thick wavy hair, extremely handsome and well sought out by the elite for the film industry. A visual artist and an amazing genius at his craft drawing pictures of an image that one would think was the real thing. Father enjoyed fishing and Genesis was blessed to go with him camping one day which was the last time that she ever saw him alive. Genesis was special from the day she was born when father noticed that a light always glowed from her eyes. However, when dad was living he spent a lot of time educating Genesis concerning her African heritage and roots. Out of jealousy of dad's love for his daughter mother took advantage of Genesis good nature and made her a slave to the brothers and sister. Mother never revealed to Dad the ancient Kemet prophecy conveying the birth of Genesis with a veil over her face. Overall, the blessed metamorphose of Genesis birth will manifest into a glorious threshold out of a carbonated embryo from a distant boundless sphere. While dad was giving Genesis a lot of attention mom was gazing at her husband with malice as he read aloud to his adolescent on the topic of roots. Somehow, mother's hatred towards Genesis caused hurtful arguments with dad which led to long and terrible disputes. Unfortunately, dad died when Genesis was about 9 years old leaving his wife widowed so, he didn't live to witness the ascending horizon of the ancient Kemet prophecy. After father transitioned from this life he left Genesis a financial inheritance which is customary in African traditions and customs. Moreover, mother was over lord of the family heirloom when Genesis was too young to benefit from the insurance policy so, she was deprived of receiving her tender. Wicked mother kept her daughter's money for herself exposing her true vicious and unacceptable actions. Then mothers envy of Genesis elevated while the young woman was growing up so, she began to think of a strategy to steal her blessings. However, mother continued using anxiety as a means of impersonating Genesis capabilities but, her schemes didn't accelerate over the magnificent young woman. Meanwhile, grandma was compelled to tell her daughter about Genesis superb nature that invigorate essentials out of the universe. Stones, crystals, cooper, gold, herbs, roots, barks, platinum, plants, trees and other elements of nature, fire, air, water earth. The building blocks or all material in existence that will impact Genesis divinity putting her on a high vibration adjoining her soul. Grandma went on to say that Genesis DNA is special and without these essentials her body will deactivate and become powerless. This blessed child can't eat unhealthy foods because it will ignite a malfunction prompting her health to collapse. Although, mothers wicked disposition overtook her and she began poisoning Genesis food and feeding her pork, beef, pasties, soda and all kinds of junk food. Genesis system couldn't combat the contaminated meals so, the circuits in her body failed and wouldn't function properly leaving her vulnerable to sickness. Otherwise, due of the aftermath of slavery Genesis African traditions and culture was not a discussion in the home during her teen years. Mother was ignorant concerning her heritage and was still impacted by the effects of slavery by fighting to protect the European way of life. However, mother tried every device that she was adept at to break Genesis and keep her from reaching her destiny believing that it's the right thing to do. Genesis lived with her mother, grandmother four brothers and a sister and they were all envious of her too. However, Genesis did share a close relationship with grandma who was a descendant from west Africa a wise woman with a brown complexion and lived in moderation. Therefore, grandma taught Genesis the importance of family and how to budget money and they were an inseparable pair. An excellent cook grandma was when people came from all over to enjoy eating her delicious meals. Grandma then taught Genesis her skills and gave her recipes but, she dies later when Genesis become 18 years old. After loving dad and Grandma departed leaving Genesis feeling abandoned with no support system which put her on dangerous ground to face her evil and dominating mother. Sadly, grandma didn't get the chance to tell Genesis about her calling concerning the ancient Kemet prophecy entailing that she was the chosen deliverer of her people. After the deceasing of loved one's mother bitterly destroy the beautiful handwoven cradle and rip up special made multi-colored cloth. The gift that was given to Genesis from grandma at birth so, she could break the spell of Kingu someday and come to know who she was. Underneath, mother's lovely exterior sheltered a demon possessed spirit that was awaiting the perfect time to act mischievously against her daughter. Therefore, mother was determined to put Genesis light out which the psychopath possessed the ability to manipulate a circumstance that fooled people. Mothers envy of the ancient Kemet prophecy became an obsession during her compulsion to punish Genesis. Overall, out of jealousy mother make Genesis a slave to the other children giving her tremendous task consolidated of constantly cooking, cleaning, and entertaining guest. Genesis brothers and sister were lazy and ungrateful with no common sense and mother didn't care she wanted Genesis waiting on them day and night. The older siblings married out of sexual and financial motivation allowing the spouse lead them away from home until times got tough and realized that they needed family after all. Instead of engaging in a relationship with someone who honored family with morals but, hooked up with a soulless one that caused a mess that wasn't easy to clean up. Genesis younger year's mother was weak, bitter, envious, her hatred was harsh, unthinkable and abusive towards her daughter making it her mission to destroy the child. All of Genesis siblings had evil spirits like mother so, she showed favor to the other children making the transition into the working world easier. Mother wanted the other children to be successful and Genesis to suffer and die as, she watched her day and night just waiting for the opportunity to get rid of her. The children were raised without their roots and exposed to European culture which is inspired through advertising conditioning the mind to make another group hero's. Whereas, black people are looked upon as niggers praising the beast when they destroy their own family unit thinking it is the right thing to do. Mother wasn't loving and had no spiritual concepts refusing to believe that it has power but, she worshiped the energy of fear while her daughter reached maturity. Mother practiced corruption all day insisting on using forces of evil, envy, greed, and hatred to rob Genesis of connecting to her divine purpose. Mother was determined to have the powers for herself not realizing that her hatred was giving Genesis more blessings by releasing karma. However, mother thought by keeping Genesis from her true essence it would deactivate her energy and stop the purpose. Now, wicked mother will find out that the divine bloodline of her daughter could not be reversed Genesis was blessed by a higher authority and will someday answer the call. Although, Genesis was a teen and the stress began to take its toll on her fragile health and emotional state. It Shattered her causing sickness where her hair began to fall out as, she noticed bald spots accumulating but her follicle gland was still active. Genesis had an irritated and upset stomach constantly after eating the poisonous food that mother fed her. However, despite what the family was putting her through she remained faithful and continued to believe that life would get better for her. It was summer when Genesis health miraculously got better and she was persistent in everything she did. Her independence acquired attention when she could hardly wait while the lack of money caused her to look for work. Therefore, Genesis galloped door to door in the community looking for whatever work she could find and she finally got work at a local restaurant cleaning. After getting paid Genesis wanted a bank account but, she was too young to open an invoice for transactions. Therefore, she kept her earnings in a rectangular shaped wooden box in the room that she shared with her older sister. Sis was tall and rather attractive with an evil demeanor and always looking for some jerk that she can use to get by. Unexpectedly, one day when Genesis went to retrieve the money that she worked hard for it was gone. Later, Genesis found out that her sister took it to help support her illegitimate children and she knew then it was time to leave her family. It was the only way to find some peace and prosperity after the two sisters battled over the loss of Genesis money. In the pretension of privacy Genesis often brained stormed about how she can make a lot of money materialize. Mother and sister continued to rob Genesis of her hard earned money causing her plans for school to fall into ruin. Instead of embracing Genesis persistence to earn money mother and sister took advantage of her generosity and robed her. Nothing was fair for Genesis but, making difficult decisions was based on the pursuit of her father's wisdom that family should never separate for material reasons. Earlier experiences that Genesis dealt with her family selfish motives taught her that single handedly greed disturbs the nature of man. It can cause a tremendous amount of stress putting a heavy strain and toll on body, mind and emotional state. Also, destroy the spiritual crown which connects you to your higher self (God) by clouding your thinking where you don't feel compassion, love or concern for others. Genesis business sense was instilled from her father so, she tried to convince her family and friends that sovereignty comes from networking in the community where you buy, sell and trade. The more Genesis petitioned with her family to go into business for themselves the worst their relationships got. When the other children were given their inheritance left by father they went on to further their education omitting considering or starting a family business. Additionally, through a study Genesis discovered that colleges were preparing students to earn wealth for corporations and not themselves and their family. Anyway, Genesis siblings were spoiled rotten, naive and deceived about mother's hidden secret of lies, fear and witchery believing the illusion that she was a good Samaritan. Mother knew that she would soon be alone with the children when they started back to school so, the grandchildren became the focus to condition for submission into immorality. The grandchildren also, inherited wicked genes so, mother privately introduced them to a witch's manual for channeling into rituals and they enjoyed it. Genesis was attractive just like her father and the center of attention causing people to stare, stalk and take pictures of her as, if she was a celebrity or someone of great worth. These people insisted on knowing who Genesis was asking personal questions given her no peace and it became frequently irritating. However, the energy Genesis released was so powerful and radiant it was natural for her to hypothesize people with her gift of charisma to get what she wanted. Despite the dysfunctional breakdown of the family Genesis knew that she had to move on for the sake of her wellbeing. However, Genesis determination was to get to the root of the problem that ruined the black class and put an end to the invasive issues. Therefore, Genesis searched for ancient occult wisdom to solve the dilemma that was plaguing the black race that led to an intense sequence of events. Meanwhile, mother didn't appreciate Genesis persistence concerning African study and insisted that she adapt to the European way of living which was customary in the family home. Generally, mother was smart in school mastering, history, geography and English possessing a wonderful and interesting talent for writing. Genesis remembered mother talking about what it was like in high school during segregation when blacks were not allowed to go to the other side of town. Mother said there were all black teachers who didn't pass students with failing grades. High school pupil's graduated mastering math, science, English, geography and African American studies were mandatory. Therefore, mother taught Genesis English instruction at home impressing her daughter who thought that mother should had been a school teacher. Mother harassed Genesis so, much about Euro-American studies and writing until she started to like putting words together and creatively. Although, Genesis questioned the system of theology and had moments when she knew that there was some good inside of mother but, she was fighting against it. Genesis exceled at all the things that she liked to do but, school was troublesome because of her special nature teachers didn't like her. Genesis enjoyed drama but, was kicked out her first day in class and couldn't even pass P.E., chorus or home make but, graduating with disappointing grades and unprepared for a future. Genesis just couldn't fit in and mother became more determined to stop her because she didn't want her daughter to stop the plan of the evil empire. However, mother was under the spell of kingu and was deceived into thinking that this civilization was the final frontier. Therefore, she laughs insanely as if there were still a chance to sabotage the ancestors plan of salvation for the oppressed people. Mother was crazy and wanted to gain control so, she contacted family in the Caribbean and Africa for assistance since they were master spiritualist. The shamans taught mother how to create a human image by using a wax figure for power and authority. Also, how to chant words over colored candles for destruction and death by giving energy over to negative forces. Then how to bury a hand sculptured coffin in the cemetery as a sacrifice to the dead by using an object of identification that will cause everything the adversary do will fail. The most used method mother was taught was to comprise a deadly formula and repeatedly extend it to the victim through a consumption of food. After mother completed her craft it was in the fall season and she called for a family gathering at their home which took place on a full moon. It was the witch's ceremony for manipulating misfortune against the subject when the infant was too young to know what was taken place. Mother will find out later that her wicked schemes was no match for the mighty power of Genesis and leads up to confusion and malevolent upheaval. Meanwhile, Genesis knew there was something wonderful on the way for her and wanted to continue her education so, she decided to tell her mother that she was going to beauty school. Mother laughs enjoying abusing her daughter saying that you are not pretty and the insult crushed Genesis but, she still wanted to go. Genesis was special and going to make something of herself but, when every door opened mother was always waiting around to close it.

Genesis goes to beauty school

Chapter 3

Genesis decide to go to beauty school to learn the concept of adequate America's idea of loveliness. At John Casablanca's Genesis develops confidence as she interacts with other students creating appealing makeovers and mastering social grace. Despite Genesis wicked mother and sister who stole the money that she earned and what her loving father tendered. However, in her early years Genesis rent a room in a large Victorian house around Flatbush avenue in Brooklyn, New York. The lodging located in the middle of a black neighborhood within a large sanctuary of businesses and surrounded by Brooklyn college. Genesis has two roommates a Jamaican girl who work as a manager for Wendy's a popular restaurant chain. As the two become friends they find themselves hanging out every moment they could grasping within their peaceful and happy abode. The other roomy was a light toned brother out of the Bronx, N.Y., and they all got along very well. Out of Genesis enormous determination to be successful in her field, she works three jobs while going to charm school. A day job at a coffee shop on a busy fast going intersection where there are much social and multi-cultural interactions. A night job at Kings plaza mall and a weekend job as a receptionist at a neighborhood real estate firm. Young vibrant Genesis had very little time for socializing while moving towards a modeling career and going without family support at all. The heavy toll of work and school began to affect Genesis health so, she started feeling ill and extremely fatigued. It was due to the lack of rest and wholesome food which forced her to take some time off. Genesis body just couldn't adjust to modern standards of a heavy work load and beauty school which became too much for her. It wasn't enough time in the day to eat healthy portions and stable meals so, Genesis ran all day and all night on an unbalanced diet. Genetically modified food was disastrous on Genesis body putting her in a desperate attempt for an immediate detox from the measurable intake of the toxins. Genesis needed to heal from the chemical intake so, she induced organic herbs, root and bark combinations for a cure. However, to maintain good health as we evolved from a natural source that didn't except dangerous synthetic applications. Includes relying on a consumption of nutritional servings which was essential for Genesis wellness for the circuits in her body to remain balanced. However, Genesis ancestors was crying out to help her but she couldn't hear them because she didn't understand the method used to summons the energy for contact. Furthermore, Genesis was eating harmful contaminated foods along with the lack of knowledge blocked communication to hear their message. Fortunately, Genesis neighbors loved her and nursed her back to good health by bringing her foods that were rich in nutrients that she needed for a full recovery. They were friends put in place who higher senses exhibited that Genesis was called for a great purpose and they dedicated themselves to help her. The neighbors knew that Genesis needed fresh electric foods (not hybrid) to activate the powerful energy within herself. Therefore, they put Genesis on a vegan diet to heal and looked in on her to make sure that she was feeling better. Since Genesis had no idea that her purpose was mandatory but, troublesome moments prepared her by forcing her into lonely, evil and unhappy places. Genesis continued to suffer on a regular basis and it just didn't seem fair that one had to endured so much while others were living with family or friends comfortable and conveniently. It wasn't normal to be under a constant attack and to such a huge degree so, Genesis decided to trace her family tree. The disclosure of the bloodline was from the ancient region of Kemet which was the root of her misfortunes brought on by an American hell. Through careful observation Genesis realized that her African roots were the most important essence of family values and stability. Therefore, it became customary for Genesis to never let another culture influence her people to live alone relocating to faraway places. Lodging where there is no protection from loved ones and making it easy to become a target by an enemy. The concept of family division certainly didn't exist in Africa and the idea is an unacceptable way of life. However, fasting was a major concern for Genesis after she consumed contaminated foods which gave her body a metamorphosis system to heal itself. Then Genesis maintained a strict vegetarian diet which was the answer for her physical recovery and wellbeing. Although, Genesis felt renewed after the healing process readying her to continue her conquering an inevitable journey. Meanwhile, there were mongrel creatures grafted during a demoralized experiment on the planet with tails that were secretly removed at birth living among the dominant species. They were strange beings appearing to be normal by pretending to possess a loving demeanor arriving on the scene using technology to access wealth and gain control. This species became familiar with Genesis earlier when mother took Genesis to a local clinic for an annual routine examination. When physicians tapped into her DNA the blood-type was o positive discovering that Genesis couldn't be immunized. This indicated that Genesis was created from a divine source that rulers were afraid of and her influence to end enemy control. The war was against carbonated beings (people of color) that are aligned with the universe and threatened the recessive gene position of authority and that was the invaders secret. They used wicked mother to assist in stopping Genesis mission because they feared the divine source of power that lurked within her. Meanwhile, unrighteous beings started using unnatural methods for power and control techniques knowing that nature wasn't on the side of a recessive gene. Scientifically, this trait was going extinct because the Sun (Ra) was entering a new cycle which wouldn't except color deficiency. Therefore, as the temperatures continue to rise and in the proper season black dominance will over throw the present ruler ship. Enemies of the universe will refuse to accept a power bigger than because they can't adapt in the cosmos so, they'll return to low light areas. However, accelerated rays from the sun's force are overwhelmingly destructive on pale subjects but, the dominant gene can produce more carbon from the sun. Earth was needed for the invaders to survive since it is the 3rd planet (dimension) from our powerful Sun in the upper atmosphere. Moreover, the new species desperately was attempted to use politics and religion as a control mechanism to dominate people and rule over them. Scientifically, hybrids are temporary and the planet would eventually return to the original owners. This knowledge was shocking for Genesis and she was in for a needed break from stress. Meanwhile, Genesis gained strength after recovering from sickness and went to visit her favorite aunt and the two were inseparable until auntie found out that Genesis was going to beauty school. Auntie became envious too and contemplated to destroy Genesis as she despised her niece for making progress. Genesis beauty and life force energy was just too over whelming for auntie so, she plotted to break Genesis spirit by trying to make her to feel hopeless. Auntie was delusional just like her sister and hired a total stranger to beat and rape Genesis by deceiving and convincing her to go on a date. After the sexual attack by her date Genesis fall into a state of shock after she got a terrible disease when crabs begin to stream down her thighs while taking a shower. Another day Genesis was walking in the neighborhood and a Rastafarian poured a bucket of water over her head after leaving the beauty parlor. Out of anger Genesis goes to the family home retrieving a knife and fastened it on her side to get revenge for the violation. When Genesis left out of the home she noticed the gang of Rasta's were hanging out at the corner store chanting and laughing. Neighbors are sitting on the stoops waiting to see the outcome of Genesis rage. She approaches the one who insulted her knowing that she was going to die because there was too many to defeat. Then Genesis grab the Rasta by the neck and threatened to slice his throat if he didn't apologize. There was an outburst from the Rasta screaming I'm sorry, I'm sorry, I'm sorry because he didn't want to die. Out of shock of the gang they considered Genesis a goddess to be honored and lifted her up in the air marching back and forth chanting hail to the queen as neighbors looked on in surprise. Due to frustration Genesis goes to the top of the two story brown stone on Vermont street in Brooklyn, New York. A rundown neighborhood and attempts to end her life by jumping off the building causing panic from the tenants. Unexpectedly, a group of religious people walked by praying persuading Genesis to decline her end and at that moment auntie asks Genesis not to come back again. Genesis became briefly homeless after having no place to go feeling hurt and completely abandoned but, she knew that she had to move on. However, she goes to the store on the block and buy a 40 ounce with a high alcohol content and while walking pushing a cart in worry. Two brothers noticed her from across the street laughing and one decided to approach her then Genesis broke the bottle over his head knocking him out cold. Then she looked at the other brother saying do you want some of this too, and he ran away in fear of his life. Meanwhile, Genesis has no idea where to go from that horrifying moment she just departed on faith. Wondering how could she sustain such stupendous strength after enduring her aunts malicious and unveiling actions. Genesis ancestors was with her the entire time for protection to uplift her through her time of tribulation. However, Genesis will to come to know that she is the chosen one who continued the challenging and obligatory journey to free her people from their miserable and deplorable bondage.

Genesis become a professional Model
Chapter 4

Genesis was strong willed so, she recovered quickly from the physical assault that she suffered by the attacker who her aunt hired to stop her modeling pursuits. However, Genesis finished beauty school and was rewarded with a list of modeling agencies that might represent her in a prestigious and exciting career. Therefore, Genesis was proud to accomplish her goal so, she began to beat the streets of New York looking for work in her field. Everywhere Genesis went agencies told her that she wasn't what they were looking for and she started running out of places listed on the directory. When Genesis got to the last resource it was a Modeling agency who told her that her look was extraordinary and commercial but, they only represented Spanish girls. Therefore, Genesis thought that her search for a professional occupation was over then unexpectedly the Spanish agency recommended a black agency that was more suitable to fit her stunning profile. The Spanish agency gave Genesis the necessary information that she needed to contact the appropriate source and she departed. A few days later, Genesis receives a phone call from the Modeling agency a black woman named Pat Evans of Pat Evans Models. Then Genesis spoke with Ms. Evans by telephone for a Dark and Lovely hair relaxer assignment in the sum of $3,000.00. Then Pat Evans introduced Genesis to the clients Lockhart and Pettus for the beauty packaging advertisement. Genesis felt fortunate that she was chosen for a new release of the product and was proud that her hard work and persistence finally paid off. Afterwards, Genesis received an appointment to meet the professional team that she would work with for the announcement of the assignment. The gathering for the job took place at a nearby beauty salon across from Bloomingdales department store within an on the go community of many businesses to entertain. Ana Fabre for hair, Reggie Wells for make-up and Tony Barboza was the photographer. Genesis underwent a fantastic hair cut at the salon that she fancied and it was noticeable by the public after leaving causing a multitude of stares. After the photography shoot with Tony Barboza he predicted that Genesis modeling career would lead to greater success in the fashion world. The team was courteous and professional and they encouraged Genesis to move ahead despite that she was an amateur. The fashion shoot was amazing and Genesis was favored for the job well done as the packaging reached stores worldwide. After, Genesis received a stupendous size check, out of her enthusiasm she engaged into a happy and monumental moment. However, in Genesis exhaustion she decided to quit her job at Kings plaza mall and the coffee shop but, she continued working for the real estate firm. Anyhow, there was a handsome young French Canadian brother name Ian who worked with Genesis and admired her on the job at the mall. After quitting her job on the way out Ian approached Genesis while she was going down the escalator asking if he could see her home. Ian was charming and a very intelligent young man who wore a very sophisticated wardrobe from fashion designer collection. Genesis was rather intimidated with his flashy wear because her style of clothing was simply composed. Ian told Genesis that he was anticipating and planning a law career and she was impressed with his remark. Therefore, she allowed him to see her home briefly discussing her professional Modeling career and Genesis had Ian's emotional support. Ian was taken by Genesis although, they had a lot in common he would follow her everywhere she went and his intensions were totally innocent. Genesis moved to Harlem, N.Y. when she lost her place in the Brooklyn college area after the property went on the market for sell. Then Genesis shared a beautiful high-rise apartment overlooking a park on Lenox Boulevard after answering a local newspaper advertisement. The roomie was a badly disfigured black male that was in love with Genesis and she didn't know it. Later, Genesis roommate realized that she really loved Ian which ended his delusional fantasy about her. Out of spite roomie then decided to poison Genesis out of jealousy causing her to become immensely sick. Genesis was then immediately rushed to Harlem hospital for medical care and the doctor discovered contamination in her bloodstream. The poison was coming from the kitchen where she exclusively ate her meals because she didn't eat out. Genesis new found love Ian protected her by raising the roommate up in the air over his head and attempting to throw him off the balcony but, was stopped by Genesis. Subsequently, Genesis recovered from the poisonous intake by the delusional maniac and Ian removed him from the apartment by threating him physically giving Genesis time find to another homestead. After the event Ian seemed to love Genesis more and the two partners needed to release stress from the anxiety that they suffered. Then they dashed onto the speedy subway and went hanging out in a night club dancing the night away. The next day these two also, enjoyed a relaxing movie at a nearby theater and visited some of the local monuments. The statue of liberty was harboring the Atlantic Ocean occupying a stunning view of the city and they also, appreciated a play at the famous Apollo theater. Then a dance performance at Alvin Ailey's Dance Theater was a rewarding experience and the next day they welcomed a day at prospect park. Submerging within a multi-racial atmosphere while delighting themselves in local entertainment as the African drum circle forged. Also, they took a long relaxing walk on Coney Island beach delighting in a fun filled amusement park while eating tasty food. The empire state building tour ended in overlooking a portion of New York City after the two healed from the painful articulated action brought on by the jealous roommate. The two found another apartment then Genesis invited her man over for dinner preparing and cooking Ian's favorite savory Mexican cuisine. However, Genesis was an excellent cook inspired by skills from grandma who passed the gift on to her granddaughter. Ian was amazed with Genesis talent for cooking and her decorative serving table so, he complimented the delicious dish. Now, Ian appreciated good tasty food and he and Genesis begin spending a lot more time together over meals. Ian was a bright young man with a promising law career in progress but, his mother took advantage of his gentle and loving nature. Therefore, when Ian was living with his family who later, became responsible for his unfortunate and deadly downfall after a jealous rendezvous. Innocent young Ian should have watched out for his mother and sister shady and tricky disposition. Later, Ian's mother met Genesis and pretended to like her by buying time while she sharpened her demonic skills to end the happy engagement. Ian's demon possessed mother came from the beautiful island of Haiti were many people say that witchcraft is commonly practiced. Ian's mother was confident that her son would be a successful attorney considering that he was spending a lot of time with Genesis who influenced him. Ian's mother was just like Genesis mother who emphasis was set on complete control over their children. His mother was determined to stop him from succeeding in law and happiness by eliminating Genesis. Anyway, Ian's love for Genesis grew and he wanted to be with her so, they decided to move in together. One day while they were asleep Genesis was visited by an ancestor in a bad dream warning her of immediate danger planned by Ian's wicked mother and sister. Genesis saw the end of her loving relationship with Ian which would put her in another position of loss. Therefore, Genesis wouldn't have the protection from a love one anymore and will survive on her on. After, Genesis woke up out of her dream she screamed franticly waking up Ian who was concerned about the bad dream. The dream revealed that Ian's mother was plotting to kill her only son by poisoning his food. Ian's mother couldn't handle the loss of dominating her son so, she deceived him into coming home for a family emergency and spiked his food with poison. Genesis couldn't say anything to Ian concerning the dream because the phone ringed and it was Ian's mother. Before Genesis answered the receiver hello, she gave Ian the phone it's your mother asking to speak with you. Ian asked her how did she know that it was mother and she responded that it's a prophetic ability that I have. After Ian hung up the phone then Genesis clairvoyant capability foresaw him going home for a family turning point and she burst into to tears. Therefore, Genesis was aware of the wicked plot behind his mother's unthinkable scheme to cause her son harm. Then Genesis mentioned to Ian if you are going to see your mother don't eat the food you must eat out. However, Genesis desperately struggled to find the words to convince Ian of the potential danger ahead of him but, he just couldn't trust it. Ian was confused concerning Genesis theory behind mother's intent to destroy her only son's happiness so, he went to visit her.

Moreover, a few days later, Genesis phone ring it's Ian saying that something was in his body and he couldn't fight it off and that she was the only one that could help him. Ian had eaten the poisonous food that his mother had given him and it made him sick after he refused to listen to Genesis warning. One afternoon Genesis encountered a second Guardian while causally walking on 42nd street in a conversation about the poisoning of Ian by his wicked mother but, it was too late. Ian didn't live much longer after the poisonous intake leaving Genesis heartbroken, alone and forsaken again. It took a long time for Genesis to recover from the ordeal so, she began drinking alcoholic beverages a lot trying to hide the pain she felt. Ian was Genesis best friend and he was gone at such a young age, her kindred spirit who shared everything including some deep and personal secrets. Genesis impression of Ian symbolized a warrior who will defend a love one at any cost and his early departure caused Genesis to cry emotionally. Soon after the horrible incident with Ian Genesis went to a local park in the mist of privacy and meditated trying to make since of what happened. Suddenly, she heard a male voice talking to her, Genesis, again Genesis a destructive attack is about to take place on American soil that will bring change to the land forever but, I'll be with you. Yes, Genesis answered with another encounter with an ancestor and at that moment she paused knowing that she is special.

Genesis goes home for a visit
Chapter 5

Genesis decided to go home trying to shine some light on what happened to Ian and deal with her family dysfunctional behavior. Although, the sociopathic and absurd bunch repeatedly engaged in dismal conduct which was a daily routine for years. Overall, there was a mental breakdown in the family who had convinced themselves to fit into European dominated society would be the best decision to live by. However, black people were determined to prove that social concepts work but, instead got taken by capitalism. It was embarrassing to see the clan selfish measures to prove to strangers who could be the most successful in the family by competing for the highest paying job. Also, who wore the fanciest cloths, lived in the most expensive home and the consequences of that mind set ruined the family. The results ended in loss, hurt, pain, suffering and division and Genesis family were conquered by an Americanized system who tricked them out of happiness. The influence Genesis family sustained in the region was bad parenting, advertising, education and leadership which was difficult to break. The hypnotic spell was associated with false images of success, money, how you should look, through media and it was enforced upon Nubian people. Meanwhile, Genesis regularly reminisced about her father's knowledge and wisdom concerning the importance of family and friends. In the early stages of her childhood Genesis father taught her that life without love is meaningless and that the people of antiquity have a compassionate nature already. Genesis father instilled in her that the indigenous people were robbed of their glorious way of life causing love to become a thing of the past. The sons and daughters of all mighty God should have never replaced their trust for the material world by impersonating demonic forces. After Genesis arrived at the family gathering it was during dinner when most of the family was there and mother raised a poisonous dosage to slip into her food. Privately, Genesis gave her mother the good news about finishing beauty school and getting accepted in a professional Modeling agency that led to her first hair assignment. Mother didn't respond to the wonderful news about Genesis success she just had a dull look on her face as if it was no big deal. Mother didn't keep the achievement of Genesis career confidential and she told her brothers and sister who felt they were left out of the spot light. Then because of jealousy they plotted against her by emphasizing their professions as if it was a competition for attention. Although, Genesis family seemed happy to see her but, she had a strange sensation as if something wasn't right. Therefore, Genesis ignored the bizarre and weird feeling because she just wanted to be home near family and friends. Afterwards, Genesis gave mother a portion of her money earned from the modeling assignment and bought herself a used reliable automobile. Then Genesis decided to go visit a girlfriend that she haven't seen in a long time who has five children living on welfare. Genesis gave her girlfriend the nickname Dawn who is also attractive, fun loving and a lightly toned young woman with average height. A talented female with aspirations of pursuing a music career but, in her efforts the occupation never materialized and later she ended up working at a daycare supervising kids. Anyway, Genesis shared her unusual experiences with Dawn concerning her journey into the modeling world. Dawn was cordial and compassionate about Genesis achievements and was happy for home girl with the best regards. Then the two friends talked about old times and hung out all night at a popular jazz spot viewed within flashy glimmering lights while socializing over cocktails. The black owned supper club specialized in healthy cuisine and was overlooking an upper floor decorated with ancient Kemet symbols surrounding the entire perimeter. Charcoal incense fragranced the atmosphere giving honor to the universal creator as it is written in the pyramid text. The concept for burning incense in African temples throughout the continent was known for enriching the environment. Incense burning was also, used in meditation to elevate divine contact and for a sleep aid to refine lucid dreams. Certain aromas enhanced the smell for attracting good energy, reversing or removing bad vibrations but, the method is more affective when surrounded by the purity of nature. However, cosmic planets or stars help to balance forces in the universe along with using aroma from incense. Burning incense impact each planet essence there is Mars the cosmic star for Aries/Scorpio and cosmic incense burned is High John the Conqueror and earth aromas. Planet Venus is the cosmic star for Taurus/Libra and the cosmic incense burned are Sandalwood. Planet Mercury is the cosmic star for Gemini/Virgo and the cosmic incense burned are Lavender and Lilly of the valley. Planet Sun is the cosmic star for Leo and incense burned are frankincense and myrrh. Planet Jupiter is the cosmic star for Sagittarius/Pieces and incense burned is lotus, honey suckle and Kush. Planet Saturn is the cosmic star for Capricorn/Aquarius and incense burned is opium. Planet Moon is the cosmic star for Cancer and incense burned is gardenia, Blue Nile, jasmine and each one are influenced by the aroma of seven African powers (Sefech Ba Ra). The essence of these seven forces exist in living beings who are affected by energy which controls unseen circumstances. Overall, at times the club showcased live entertainment featuring Kemet belly dance performances enacted by solo African drummers. The dancers wore a bra and belt sequin which was attached to a colorful hip scarf and matching coined necklace. Wrist cuffs, gold hair bands, beaded accessories and beautiful veils dancing throughout the isles were amusing. As guest socialized over cocktails and waitresses roamed about the social club selling metaphysical items. Dawn was impressed by the club atmosphere making a remark that this is different from the R/B days. Genesis responded we as a people of color need change culturally also, embrace our African culture and traditions regularly. Dawn was confused about what to order on the menu so, Genesis ordered a vegetarian curry stew, minced coriander and a cup of fresh fruit for the two then Dawn commented on how delicious the meal was. Genesis spoke, we need a healthy diet and teach our children better eating habits that compliments the culture. Altogether, get rid of the fast food, honor our customs, bring home our children from distant places and stop celebrating holidays that don't reflect on us as a special class of people. Also, we should home school or private school our children so, they can get their heritage and curriculums that will better prepare them for the future. Dawn responded, wow! You must be chosen for something great then the evening ended and Genesis returned to mother's house. Then a few days later, Genesis receives a phone call for another professional modeling assignment. A jewelry advertisement for Avon for their monthly campaign issue in the sum of $1000.00. Afterwards, Genesis forge into an introduction with an important client for the company who was a Jewish man name Barry. He liked Genesis look and personality then immediately wanted her for Avon's next issue. Therefore, Genesis met and hooked up with the make-up and wardrobe team who enjoyed working with her. The jewelry photo shoot was a successful accomplishment and was in next month's magazine subscription. Telephone calls continued coming in for more professional Modeling assignments and the next one for a Bacardi rum poster advertisement. The amount was in the tender of 25,000. and Genesis began building a professional portfolio to show off. However, Genesis gave mother photos of her professional modeling ads. thinking that she would be proud but, instead behind Genesis back the pictures was disposed in the garbage. Despite how Genesis was hurt and mistreated by her jealous and pitiful family she loved her mother and wanted her to be happy. Genesis kept a portion of the money that she earned and the other portion she took her mother on a trip to Atlantic city because mother enjoyed taking chances gambling on slot machines. Everyone was grown-up working in their profession and adding additional clan to the family tree except for that next to the oldest spoiled crack head brother who totally depended on mother for everything. Out of fear of loneliness mother became demanding and controlling in the home when the loss of a close male companionship ended in death. Mother took it out on Genesis and her hatred grew deeper against her daughter making it impossible to break the spell. Suddenly, Genesis received another call from the modeling agency accepting an assignment for a huge amount of $25,000. for a commercial. Nervousness set in because Genesis had never done television work before and she failed the screen test but, the clients still wanted her for the job. Therefore, the patrons offered to send Genesis to television commercial classes and she was pleased to honor the arrangement. Although, television commercial classes didn't come easy for Genesis but after taking a second screen test she passed. Afterwards, Genesis was told by the Modeling agency to be on stand-by for the assignment and she waited patiently. Genesis didn't realize that mother was against her Modeling and was secretly planning to sabotage the career by waiting closely by the phone. Wicked mother couldn't control her dysphoria and she was determined to stop Genesis from getting the commercial so, her daughter could join in on her misery. Therefore, mother began attacking Genesis emotionally, physically and mentally by yelling, screaming and hitting her intensely. Mother was malicious and concentrated heavily on using negative feedback to ruin Genesis reliable reputation. Also, mother would instigate false allegations against Genesis creating an uncomfortable situation for her supporters. Telephone calls for Modeling assignments ended when mother privately told Genesis agent several times that she was not available and gave deceitful reports against the young woman. Genesis was scared and confused by mother's actions and went to confronted Dawn about the horrible conduct induced by mother actions concerning her Modeling career. Genesis best friend Dawn responded by saying you know that your mother and my mother never was good to us. I believe that this ridiculous acquisition is not acquitted and we're going to get to the bottom of these issues. Genesis spent a few days with Dawn trying to figure out what was happening with her mother. Suddenly, Dawn's brother Shante came by for a visit and they mentioned to him what Genesis mother was doing against her. Then Genesis told Dawn's brother it was just like she said as Genesis began seeing floating small objects moving about the room and no one else could see them.

Those objects are alerting you said Dawn's brother about something is coming to surface. Dawn didn't have a phone so, the two best friends looked at each other rushing off towards Genesis mothers house to call the Modeling agency. After reaching mother's house Genesis made the phone call while Dawn was listening in on the phone in another room. Hello, Ms. Evan's from the Modeling agency answering...where are you, I been trying to contact you for days for the television commercial can you get here in a few minutes. Genesis responded, in a few minutes there is no way I can get there quickly I'm a long distance from you. Agent say's, the clients have been waiting for you and if you can't make it right now we have a replacement to take your place. Genesis responded to her agent what's going on Ms. Evan's why do you want to replace me. The agent responded to Genesis I been calling you for day's leaving messages with your mother. However, she told us terrible things about you that you were on drugs and that you were always in trouble with the police so, the clients made the decision to replace you. Genesis answers what! then the agent Ms. Evan's was in disbelief that Genesis mother could spread bad rumors about her daughter then the phone hangs up. Dawn replies to Genesis so, that's what mother was up to and that's messed up you worked so hard without any support from anyone. That is demonic how your mother waited after you worked three jobs and finished school to become a professional Model then deliberately destroy your career. You Shared your wages with your mother who didn't love you and in return mother robed you of everything. Genesis cried miserably knowing that family would never be the same again but, insisted that she still deserve better. Painfully, responding to Dawn, I need to be alone right now the tension was taking a toll on Genesis in the unforgivable action. Afterwards, the doors to the modeling world remained closed and never opened again after Genesis reputation was badly damaged.

Genesis Health Fails
Chapter 6

Shortly, after Genesis lost the Modeling career her health began to fail again and she started going to her doctor on a regular basis complaining about stomach upset. The medical physician couldn't find anything wrong with Genesis but, she continued to complain. During a visit with her doctor Isla Jayden who has a good standing and reputation concerning medical wellness asked Genesis to see a psychotherapist. A colleague of Doctor Jayden name Doctor Dekel in her occupational medicine group was asked to help determine the cause of Genesis medical apprehensions. Genesis asked her Doctor why should she see a shrink and Doctor Jayden responded you seem to have some emotional issues to address when your physical examination was normal. Doctor Jayden suggested that a psychotherapist will be the proximity we need to find your health concerns to diagnosis a resolution. Genesis answered, Doctor Jayden again in disbelief your telling me that you want me to see a shrink doctor. Yes, because you are constantly complaining about an upset stomach and I can't find anything that suggests your discomfort so, I believe that there may be some emotional distress at stake. Genesis collaborates with Doctor Jayden and make an appointment for a further study and go to see Doctor Dekel the psychotherapist. Afterwards, Genesis met with the psychotherapist office receptionist who were waiting for her and she said the Doctor is ready for you now. Doctor Isabell Dekel came out and introduced herself, hello Genesis how are you o.k. thanks replies Genesis. The physician spoke to Genesis your primary medical Doctor Jayden told me what's going on with you. Lay down on the coach and tell me everything that you can remember about yourself since you were a youngster. After Genesis explained to the psychotherapist that she had a rough childhood and that she was treated unfair and punished for doing good. My brothers and sister were rewarded and praised for doing wrong and mother deliberately sabotaged my professional Modeling career spreading lies and rumors that I'm incompetent. After Genesis showed the psychotherapist her modeling portfolio she was immediately diagnosed with traumatic stress disorder. Genesis asked the doctor what does that mean and doctor Dekel said it's when your mind and body goes through a break down by a frightening experience that cause you to become physically ill. Genesis cries emotionally while the Doctor asked if she could have a meeting with her along with mother. Genesis laughs repeatedly, my mother will never come to your office and admit to the horrible and shameful things that she has done and said against me. Doctor Dekel answers, I'm going to call your mother to set up an appointment and get to the root of your sickness and get you started on the road to recovery. Doctor Dekel goes on to say that it's so, unfortunate for you Genesis and not fair when your mother completely manipulated the circumstance at your expense. Genesis responded my mother will never talk to you Doctor Dekel but, the Doctor insisted on calling mother anyway. Ring, hello this is Doctor Isabell Dekel who is calling on behalf of your daughter Genesis then the phone dies and Genesis responded. I told you Dr. Dekel my mother will never admit to the terrible things that she has done to me well, I will send your primary care doctor my final diagnosis. Meanwhile, Genesis returned to see her primary care physician and the receptionist spoke, the Doctor will see you now. Dr. Jayden explained to Genesis that her colleague Dr. Dekel gave a finished diagnosis of your health. We recommend that you cut off all ties with mother and Genesis answered but, why Doctor Jayden. Then Dr. Jayden told Geneses that mother was astutely killing her so, to continue undergoing stress, suffering, sickness and death is the result. Doctor Jayden persisted to tell Genesis I'm so, sorry to say it but, your mother doesn't love you and doesn't deserve you. Then Genesis knew she had to somehow get pass the unfortunate and inevitable set of circumstances. Therefore, she had to remove herself from horrible mother that was demoralizing her credibility. Months had gone by and Genesis continued to be sick, her illness was worst causing her to be confined to a bed and for a long time. Genesis was trying to use her will power to break the spell of negative forces that mother used when she was poisoning her food that made her sick. Genesis don't believe that witchcraft has power over magic but, her second eldest brother felt compassion for her and insisted it was an act of witchery. Now, mother was giving Genesis alcohol rubs while looking in on her from time to time pretending to be concerned about her failing health. Hoping that she has Genesis where she wanted her to obliterate her and finish her off once and for all. Mother deceived Genesis trying to take advantage of stealing her blessing that was conveyed by grandmas ancient Kemet prophecy. Meanwhile, Genesis begin to gain some strength and needed a break from the uncertainty that she was facing with her health. Therefore, Genesis decided to go for a drive towards east Saint Louis, Missouri hoping that an adventure would help her to heal. Along the travel a bad intuition occurred when running over an animal that she couldn't avoid. Although, Genesis couldn't explain the incident and continued to drive but, she insisted on going hoping for renewal. It was during the summer when Genesis arrived and quickly she noticed the famous arch monument over-looking the river front park. The beautiful scenery led Genesis to explore the recreational grounds as she observed the outdoor performing theater while fireworks set off at night. Trendy clothing shops were plentiful while Genesis mingled among the crowd and there were still many burnt out buildings left from the riot of 1917. Genesis befriended a local couple who suggested that she have dinner at BB's Jazz Blues & soup Lounge in downtown St. Louis. The supper club specialized in Cajun and creole dishes which was very delicious. After dinner Genesis took a chance on welcoming good fortune at the Lumiere Place Casino Hotels within a cathedral style interior. The busy casino was filled with cocktail bars, slot machines, roulette and card tables to occupy. However, the Agua Lounge section of the business performed live entertainment attracting tourist from all over the country. Early the next day Genesis went on a tour of the city of east St. Louis embarking on old burnt out buildings left from the riots. It was a time when an outbreak of labor and race relations led to violence killings of over 200 local citizens causing major property damage on the banks of the Mississippi river. The riots sparked when thousands of Caucasian men attacked black workers resulting into tension, injuries and caused many deaths. The aftermath ended in a bloody massacre that left thousands of black families to fall into homelessness. The riot was known as one of the worst catastrophic events of the 20th century in American history. Although, Genesis could still feel the racist energy lingering over the city where the incident took place decades ago. The next morning Genesis departed from east St. Louis heading back to mother's house feeling better from the stress she that she had undergone.

Genesis opinion of legendary east Saint Louis was a place to visit full of professionals and everyday working decent people. Then she departed from the historical city exiting onto the highway viewing gorgeous mansions and villa's. When Genesis galloped along the road after she enjoyed a needed adventure and relaxing drive. Shortly, after propelling onto the countryside of Missouri's manors out of the rear mirror when she observed an older Caucasian man. He was fast approaching in an old huge solid unyielding vehicle which continuously attacked her car causing her to spin off the road. The vehicle flipped over and over crushing the car tossing Genesis out of the car front window. She landed into a bean patch and was nearly killed but, she was quickly rescued by a passing truck driver. The truck driver called an ambulance that took Genesis to a nearby hospital where she received immediate medical attention. The emergency room diagnosis was mild wounds and just a few scratches to Genesis left shoulder and arm then she was released the same day. The hospital transported Genesis to a local hotel where her family arrived but, unfortunately the assailant was never found. After returning home mother gave Genesis alcohol rubs pretending she was concerned about the accident by taking advantage of her innocence. During that night mother fell asleep and received a visit in her dream from a protector of Genesis. The guardian demanded that she remove the curse that she placed on her daughter or suffer the consequences of a harsh punishment. Out of fear of the dream mother proceeded to lift the curse by given Genesis a root to take that broke the affliction.

Genesis starts her own business
Chapter 7

Early the next day after the car accident Genesis was in bed watching a television program concerning starting your own business. The course was about how to be self-employed selling products and Genesis was mesmerized by the anticipated concept. Instantly, an adrenaline outburst of powerful energy increased into Genesis body causing her to miraculously feel better. The root that mother gave Genesis released a divine source of healing and chased away the demonic forces that were plaguing her. Uplifting and taking Genesis into an adventurous odyssey that she could possibly take on and conquer the world perpetually. After Genesis lost her Modeling career she had to find a way to quickly accumulate money because mother was still typically waiting in her crafty and shrewd manner to annihilate her. Mother was desperately after her daughter's blessing but, she was cautioned by the dream which demanded the release of Genesis soul. Doctor Jayden warned Genesis of the potential danger opposed on her by mother and suggested that she get away from her or she could die. Genesis continued to observe the self-employed program on television while planning to hurtle into a new found an unfamiliar profession. Therefore, Genesis went to a local wholesale distributor that she found by glimpsing in a local newspaper and rush to the commerce to purchase products out of anxious despair. After doctor bills piled up Genesis had $10.00 left so, upon arrival at the community market she noticed cologne valued at $1.00 each. Genesis purchased 10 bottles costing her $10.00 giving her a total of ten packaging's of fragrance. She assembled the merchandise and took the bottles of the sweet aroma and pushed the bouquet on the street. Genesis sold all 10 bottles of perfume in nearly one hour at $10.00 each giving her the sum of $100.00. The achievement encouraged her to continue selling the product and she went door to door. Genesis thought to herself Wow! I'm making good money selling cologne and returned to the wholesale market. She then purchased $100.00 in fragrance at a $1.00 each selling the product proficiently and effortlessly earning a total of $1000.00. Out of Genesis pursuit of wretchedness she turned to Dawn who is out of work introducing the business of a self-employment based on commission sells. Considering that the two have a lot in common immediately Dawn agrees to the terms and they emerged into the door to door small enterprise. Later, Dawn mentions to Genesis if she would be interested in bringing two other sisters on board of the company Jade and Deka. Jade is a short and cute but, rather slow moving young woman who shared a low-income apartment with her mom and younger brother. Deka was heavy set, aggressive, daring, always laughing and she and Dawn was from the same hood. After Genesis met the potential workers and explained the business proposition she hires the young women immediately. Then Genesis train the young women in sales putting Jade in charge of administration because of her knowledge of accounting. Deka in sales because she accumulated a high volume of accounts in the business giving the company a needed boost. Genesis was a natural for making her own money and started sewing women's garments and crafting jewelry to add to the line. Just when Genesis thought that she had reached her fate suddenly, her employees were influenced by outsiders and told to get a real job then everyone quits. Meanwhile, Genesis former employees embarked on the corporate world where there was no freedom and the wages was low, then asking Genesis to take them back and she refused because of unprofessionalism. In Genesis younger years she remembered reading a book about the Willie Lynch speech that was addressed to a welcoming audience on the bank of the James river in Virginia in 1712. The lecture demonstrated to other slave owners how to affectively control their black slaves. The speech captivated the audience by a successful method of protocols discovered through separating one slave against the other. The technique had Genesis convinced that the problem with today's black people not coming together is an act of Willie Lynch's slave owner system. When the house nigger is against the field nigger and still the method has an impact on black people today. Shortly, Genesis loses her friend Dawn after welfare ended then she developed a pattern of living with unwedded men. These men were possessive and dominating and influenced Dawn to desert the business leaving Genesis on her own. Meanwhile, one sunny day Genesis was on her way to mother's house after grocery shopping and along the way she met a young man from the neighborhood name Damien. Damien was a mama's boy that lived in a simple house with his mother but, his father was a hard worker who tried to raise him to be a man. Damien bought a huge amount of fragrance from Genesis showing interest in the product and they started a brief conversation about how it can be marketed. Damien seemed to be a nice person with a generous personality but, yet a little slow, uncoordinated, tall, unattractive and timid. Genesis briefly mention to Damien that she needed to move towards earning big profits for the business. Therefore, Damien offered to help and Genesis appreciated the clumsy uncoordinated guy and she took advantage of the opportunity to build a potential business. After Genesis explained the business to the awkward young man she asked him if he would publicize and retail her cologne. Damien was anxious to get to know Genesis so, he decided to give the product a try. After he quickly sold out of the first batch of cologne he was completely convinced to work for her. Damien was intimidated by Genesis amazing beauty and wit and he kept it a secret that he wanted her. However, Genesis wasn't aware that Damien was bewitched by her charm, she was just focused on making the business a success. The two set a time to meet later to organize their next crusade and Genesis went to mother's house. When Genesis got home she began planning how to work together with Damien to raise the money needed to sustain herself. Therefore, Genesis had to act quickly because wicked mother found out about her business adventure and tried to stop her by calling the police. When the police arrived at Genesis mother's residence she told law enforcement that she wanted that business of selling stopped. The police told mother that selling products was not a crime and they looked at Genesis with pity and they left. Everything Genesis achieved, valued or envisioned mother was always somewhere around waiting to spoil and demise her. Mother found out that Genesis had one delinquent payment on her Toyota after receiving a call from the dealership. Genesis only had a few payments left on the 12,000 vehicle so, out of spite mother insisted that Toyota repossess the automobile to prevent Genesis from doing business. Genesis was young and unfamiliar with contracts not realizing that her car couldn't be impounded by missing one payment. However, Genesis didn't pursue the issue because she simply wasn't aware that the dealership wrongfully repossessed the car to put on the market for resale. Due to Genesis ignorance of the repossessed automobile she spent the money she earned and payed cash to purchase another vehicle. After the embarrassing incident with the repossessed car, Genesis knew that she had to work harder to remove herself from dysfunctional mother who was committed to holding her back. Then Damien begin witnessing the shocking, evil and bizarre episodes against Genesis so, he volunteered to sell her fragrance day and night to help her get out of her mother's house. The sales were going well but, uncoordinated Damien was disturbingly attracted to Genesis and could not impede from wanting someone of her caliber and standing. Another, day Genesis was taking a coffee break and someone who she did business with approached her about Damien secretly selling pornography on disc. Out of surprise Genesis confronted Damien concerning the report then his manhood felt threatened and his disposition became arrogant towards her. Suddenly, Damien becomes obsessed with watching pornography and selling the filthy videos while maliciously waiting for the opportunity to take advantage of Genesis. The two had been working together for a long time and Genesis thought that she had Damien's assurance until one day he invited her over for dinner. Genesis had no idea that Damien was disconnected from reality when he was raised in a Christian background so, she accepted the invitation. Crazed Damien put sleeping pills in Genesis drink after she made a trip to the restroom and when returning to her meal she passes out unconsciously. Damien then becomes possessed demonically and rapes her leaving Genesis to wake up discovering that her legs was elevated against the wall while her uterus and buttocks had been penetrated. Genesis now astutely declared Damien an evil sick person and betrayer of good because he didn't have what it took to succeed. While in shock Genesis concluded that Damien's intentions were take control of the situation causing her to feel powerless by exploiting her femininity. After the alarming violation of Genesis body one would think that Damien would have considered how much she had suffered already. However, the attack of Genesis by Damien was painful and if she didn't leave the neighborhood quickly she might murder the deranged, hopeless and soulless guy. Genesis then went to the library and stumbled across a book on locking hair and discovered that wooly growth is called 9 Ether. Therefore, Genesis studied the texture of wooly hair and the type is the highest number in the universe which is connected to the supernatural world that look like the top of a tree (cosmic) and is an extension to nervous system. Carbon produces color and the 9 Ether characteristic of a person who function at the highest capacity of each one but, other species are hybrids. The dark gene type has been polluted over time and compromised by sickness, disease, viruses bought on consuming genetically modified food and mutation causing molecular damage. Manifesting cancer, autism, bipolar, blood diseases like anemia and leukemia and others. However, Genesis went into further research which entailed the existence of a supreme and oxidized (change) race of green descendants called the Anunaki (9 ether beings). The Anunaki left tablets of Adapa (Adam), the first man to remind the aboriginal people that they came from a bloodline of greatness. A lineage made in their image but, the children of antiquity can't remember because of the spell of Kingu. Furthermore, out of that astonishing revelation Genesis went to see an Loctician and locked her hair. She then returned to mother's house to find out that the windows were closed, locks were changed, telephone number too and was told by mother that she didn't care whether she lived or died. Out of the hard work that Genesis put in and with little rest she was robbed of all her plans. Mother deliberately ruined Genesis by destroying her modeling career, business and she had no idea where to go from there or the had the strength to go on. Genesis took what she had and hit the road going place to place sometimes in unsafe and perilous surroundings. Although, Genesis was raised to forgive people who commit sin against another and just ask Jesus to forgive them and they will automatically receive salvation. However, it finally became a reality that Genesis was taught to worship white supremacy and people who don't have a conscious can't be rehabilitated. Genesis wasn't sure if she could sustain herself after such a tremendous blow but, rather transition from this life than acknowledge family or friends who honor demonic forces.

Genesis meet an African spiritualist
Chapter 8

No matter what happened to Genesis she refused to look back insisting that she wasn't responsible for the terrible actions of others. In her determination to start a new life based on positive pursuits while trying to upholding safety precautions. Genesis needed to be stronger than ever as she felt much restraint after the loss of her Modeling career and abandon with nothing but, faith. The sexual assault by her employee Damien who violated her and the hatred undergone by her family was more than she could bare. Meanwhile, after Genesis removed the extremist from her capacity and took on another incentive while she went on the road going place to place. The first stop was Atlantic City, New Jersey surrounding one of the most recognized boardwalks on the beach in the united states. The resort was known for fun on the sand filled with daily activities, five star hotels and restaurants. The view of the sunrise and sunset was a pleasant moment to experience while Genesis walked along the sandy sea shore. However, she observed masses of people surfing, fishing, parasailing or just enjoying a relaxing cruise on the ocean. Afterwards, Genesis glimpsed at the bright lights surrounding the busy casino's which was filled with multi-racial crowds. Altogether, she sipped on free cocktail's while enjoying an outdoor concert and festival performed by well-known entertainers. Then Genesis galloped up and down the active shopping strip hanging out in trendy clothing outlets and shops before sheltering laughs at a local comedy spot. The next adventure Genesis experienced was Philadelphia where she visited local museums and aquariums. Wine tasting on the river and long walks through enchanted gardens was relaxing after a tour of the academy of fine arts. That night Genesis went to The Laff House, a black owned comedy club located at 1412 chestnut street, 19146. Genesis glanced at photos of famous comedians that performed at the club on the wall and sipped on cocktails that were affordably priced. The host of the opening act was hilarious making jokes of the audience that sat up close to the stage. That night the club featured Bill Bellamy and Paul Mooney live on stage and Genesis took notice that families and friends were enjoying a good time. After a night sleep Genesis went to "The African American museum" in Philadelphia that celebrated black writers of literary events which circulated throughout the United States. There were photos of influential Philadelphia natives and author readings featuring the life and work of African American heritage and culture. Galleries were filled with rich history, art and a video presentation to finalize the production. Later, Genesis eased on down the road to Washington D.C. to well-known spots in the black community known for business and entertainment. Nightlife was packed at clubs and lounges where LOVES was one of the largest party hangouts in the nation accommodating famous stars and professionals. Georgia avenue was the famous strip enclosing African American bookstores and poetry theaters which surrounded Howard university. Genesis wanted a meal so she went to the Dukem Ethiopian restaurant and apple lounge, 1110 U Street NW, Washington, D.C. 20009. A popular vegetarian spot with prices ranging between 11.00 to 30.00 dollars which served generous portions of ethnic flavors, spices, lentil dishes, stews and with wonderful hospitality. After Genesis left the restaurant she went to the National Museum of African American History. Where you learn about the richness and diversity of the African American experience transcending the boundaries of race that divided us commemorating and celebrating freedom. There were collections of artifacts, documents and artwork, books and manuscripts that reflects black culture. Genesis last stop was the Black Fox Lounge, 1723 Connecticut Avenue, NW Washington D.C. 20009. A contemporary atmosphere and comfortable setting to transact business serving International cuisine by an executive chef soliciting wines from all over the world. Live jazz was the supper club main attraction emphasizing local talented musicians accompanied with soft delicate piano, blues, soul, R/B, bass combo's and guitar solo. The supper club has two levels to accommodate small, medium and large conferences. After departing from D.C. Genesis drove towards Los Angeles prepared to stay one month but, ended up staying for three years. After arriving she visited the downtown fashion district located on 9th and Olympic which is a popular shopping spot for tourist. Santee Alley was a sectional area of the busy market place filled with imported goods from all around the world. Leimert park was a community built in the 1920's consolidating historical and contemporary African American art, music and culture. Jefferson park which was north and Vermont square east of Hyde park, South Windsor Hills, Crenshaw west in the upper middle class neighborhoods. Composed of mostly black residents flourishing in blues, jazz clubs and venues for hip hop, theatres and poetry readings. The longest running hip hop open mic in the world and a popular place for performances and gatherings. Genesis was fascinated by the African drum circle that convenes every weekend but, she noticed that every time brothers and sisters got together to enjoy a peaceful function Caucasian police would come to break it up. Then Genesis arrived at fox hill mall and was captivated by sexy clothes when glimpsing through the window of shops which was showcased by dancers on soul train episodes. Conscious gear was Genesis forte so, she visited little Ethiopia to purchase clothing of her choice and next door to the Jewish thrift shop. Santa Monica and Venus beach was a long stretch of boardwalk combined where local vendors would set-up to display their merchandise. On the famous beach in southern California's main tourist attraction stretched nearly one and a half miles of long manicured sand surfacing on the Pacific Ocean. There were people roller skating, recreational volleyball took place, all types of souvenirs were sold, suffering, there were fortune tellers, juice and cocktail bars was in place, clothing stores, tattoo artist, mimes, jugglers, break dancing, weight lifting, arts and crafts sold within a huge demographics of diversity. Also, a huge amusement park on the white sandy beach pushing tides to fluctuate into the turquoise blue ocean which was the tourist playground. In downtown Los Angeles, Ca. there were regular bus schedules going to the beach which serviced 24 hours a day to transport visitors to all day fun. Then there was a stunning view of the legendary Hollywood sign implanted on mount Lee in the Santa Monica mountains which is 45 feet tall and 350 feet wide with white capital letters made in 1923. The advertisement was overlooking the city and the Hollywood walk of fame was within the series sidewalks. Famous personalities were placed along the busy avenue who made contributions to the entertainment industry. Long streets occupied blocks of movie theaters, restaurants, nightclubs, hotels, radio stations, clothing shops was positioned on the red metro train line. Genesis was wrenched to the movie studio tour where paramount, Sony, universal and warner brothers were the main attraction. The journey into the world of imagination energized Genesis for the the Bates motel, the wizard of Oz, men in black tour were just a few. The production consisted of television shows like jeopardy and wheel of fortune as the main draw although, the events were fit for applause and was just a fantasized high. There were mantled blocks on four acres of land of the historic sites laughing along with the famous comedian of the tonight show starring Jay Leno. Genesis enjoyed award winning King Kong in 3-D, the plane crash of War of the Worlds, Norman Bates at the legendary Bates Motel and jaws under the water. Genesis next travel adventure was Chicago where she lived for nearly a year and visited the black ensemble theater, one of the nation's top in performances showcasing African American professional artist. Close by was the Signature lounge located at 875 W. Michigan Ave. Chicago, IL, 60611 on the top floor of the John Hancock Tower. The club was overlooking an impressive scenery of downtown that was the perfect romantic setting by the window where the ambience of dress was casual. Drinks were expensive nearly $15.00 dollars which was out of Genesis budget but, she ordered and sipped on a cinnamon chai cocktail that was deliciously worth it. There were many downtown night clubs for entertainment in Lincoln park located in a diverse atmosphere of Brazilians, Greeks, blacks, and Caucasian. Club "The Bottom" was where musicians performed live while the staff gave excellent service and drinks were reasonable priced. There were many museums of contemporary art but, Genesis favorite was the "DuSable". The museum featured African American art a dedicated study and conservation highlighting professional black artists. The museum emphasized a collection of Ida b. Wells, violin of poet Paul Lawrence Dunbar. Including works from W.E.B Dubois, sociologist St. Clair Drake, poet Langston Hughes displaying over 13,000 artifacts, books, photo's, art and memorabilia of these scholars. Lake Michigan beach had wonderful scenery of downtown Chicago skyscrapers where you can take a river cruise and enjoy the cities architecture. The ocean shore was a fun place to hang-out or relax with your partner watching volleyball tournaments, air shows, water shows or just spending time with family and friends. As the year ended Genesis departed from Chicago and returned to her favorite geographical area N.Y.C. which was her forte. The city was known for the Hustlers paradise and triumphing enormously in business and the entertainment arena. After launching onto the highway towards the east coast Genesis slept in the car at rest stop along the way. At one stop Genesis noticed an approaching police officer who asked to see her identification and mentioned if anyone might be looking for her. Then the police officer seemed sad to hear about Genesis family neglect before releasing her. After arriving it was a rewarding experience grinding day and night selling products independently after losing the modeling career. Although, business was slow Genesis needed financial assistance and thought because of her generosity in helping others that she might receive some compensation. Then earlier, when Genesis regularly communicated with family and friends and her finances were plenty she tremendously supported her sister and children. When sis went through a separation Genesis bought her and the children into her home rent free but, after the situation got better they totally forgot Genesis and had her falsely arrested. Then, Genesis blessed her youngest brother too, with $1,000 towards a down payment on a mortgage that he engaged in with a Caucasian female. The family was alien to the woman and the stranger took advantage of his stupidity then got rid of him and ended up with the property. Genesis helped her siblings financially to accomplish their aspirations but, unfortunately when she needed support they chose to help friends and neighbors while waiting to watch Genesis fall. Anyhow, the family was jealous of Genesis and wasn't concerned that she was there for them when they were in need. Therefore, Genesis felt sorry for anyone who met this clan of soulless people because they would be cursed and marked for distress. The biggest hardship Genesis faced was that her heart was broken from an overload of stress endured by family resulting in a long time to recuperate. Meanwhile, Genesis took one day at a time handling constant losses, inconveniences, frustrations and disappointments and she couldn't afford an apartment at that time. Therefore, renting room to room was Genesis only option answering ads. in local newspapers and the most common ethnic publication in New York was the Amsterdam news. Genesis also, searched the internet for other findings and the experience was unacceptable when renters were somewhat eccentric. Asking private questions concerning her personal life and entering her room illegally looking through belongings was an audacious act violating her stay. One busy afternoon while Genesis were selling her products a middle aged black man who was a regular customer knew a friend that had an apartment for rent in Jamaica, Queens. He gave Genesis the address and she went to see the place out of despair she takes the apartment. Genesis thought that her misfortunes were over but, later she discovered that the apartment was illegal and she had to prepare to move again. After taking advantage of the unlawful rental Genesis saves some cash after six months of living free and moved to Elisabeth, New Jersey. There she took on a room with a private bath and after moving in Genesis was complaining about bed bugs and an infestation of mice. The slum lord was a Caucasian average size older man with white hair who became fascinated with Genesis and gave her a creepy feeling. When Genesis ignored him he deliberately planned to harm her by illicit entering her room and spraying it with pesticides causing her to get seriously sick. She was taking to the hospital emergency room by ambulance and was told to call her family because the doctors might not be able to save her but, there was no family to contact. During recovery in her room Genesis witnessed Caucasian tenants who were falling months behind in rent and giving the opportunity to catch up. However, when black people defaulted on one month payment the landlord filed for an eviction. After Genesis healed from the poison intake she requested a hearing concerning the deadly action to the courts. She explained how the landlord put her in a bad demise but, the soulless judge ruled in the owner's favor. After the injustice regarding the poisoning, Genesis responded to another advertisement rushing to move out from the wicked owner who attempted to kill her. She then excepted a brown skinned Jamaican girl for a roommate in East Orange, N.J. who used the rent to buy drugs and entertain quest then threatens Genesis for not excepting the bull. Genesis quickly moved again in a transitional peril into a temporary room in Crown Heights, Brooklyn because of the tremendous attacks stress was taking a toll on her body causing her to ovulate exhaustion. Genesis then questioned unanswered prayer as her will to survive became more difficult wondering why god wasn't avenging the terrible circumstances. Therefore, out from the earthly hell raised up the living dead who was constantly after Genesis soul wanting her to suffer because she was a daughter of the universal creator. These beings were against righteousness and chose to live ungodly lives and wanted Genesis to join them. After surviving the victimization Genesis continued to beat the streets of New York and New Jersey selling her products hoping that a change for better will soon come. Genesis was barely maintaining the rent then one day while selling the products in East Orange, New Jersey she noticed a special decorated store front. However, Genesis decided to enter the business thinking there might be some answers to her constant adversity. While glancing through the window Genesis observed some Kemet statues and out of curiosity she rang the bell. The women of African descent opened the door fully dressed in conscious wear and mentioned that she was expecting her. Genesis was cautious thinking the spiritual practice might be a gimmick but, out of desperation for better she entered the door. Hello, a strange looking woman spoke out asking Genesis to have a seat offering to buy some products and discuss her future. Talk to me Genesis said to the shaman then the healer asked if she could purchase some products and volunteered to tell Genesis about her beloved birth. However, the African spiritualist revealed to Genesis that she was born with a veil over her face meaning that she was the chosen one for the better of the aboriginal people. Your birth was very special the healer goes on to convey to Genesis and you will experience some upcoming events that will change your life forever. Genesis was moved by the African shaman's comment while she continued to say it was winter when you were an infant and a family gathering occurred. Your mother performed an evil ceremony against you when you were born trying to reverse your blessing and take the powers of for herself. The veil symbolizes your family tree that is rooted from galactic energy up among the assembly of spectacular stars. The descendants are beings called the Anunnaki (Nibiru) from the 12th planet who orbits throughout the solar system. These beings are more advanced in technology, mathematics, astronomy and bought knowledge to this civilization. Therefore, the offspring of this bloodline was closer to the Sun enhancing pigment but, those who have a color deficiency is better off away from the Sun's force because it can be destructive. Meanwhile, Adam (Adapa) didn't come to know good and evil by biting an apple, it was when the Anunnaki mixed their DNA with Caucasian DNA creating Demigods and the body structure changed. It angered other Anunnaki's who didn't approve of mixing genes because of the breakdown from a RH-POSITIVE FACTER. Overall, those who deliberately mix interracially transitioned to another planet to be void of this type of concept. However, the African shaman spoke mentioning to Genesis that the chemistry in your bloodline is related to the creator of the universe. Although, your ancestors who established this civilization developed it when Africa was one mass of land and structure on the planet. Those descendants were the original witnesses of the creation until they began calling on another god. This angered the all mighty God who later decided to separate the species and divide the gigantic African land mass into sectional territories. The terrestrial beings quickly multiplying on the earth but, the supreme hierarchy had a different plan apart from the homeland. The species was to be briefly on the planet because they didn't anticipate the importance of nature as a source of life. The shrewd beings knew that to govern society would someday fail and they would have to depend on the indigenous people for solutions to solve the decline. Although, the salvage beast worked around the clock to prevent brothers and sisters from awaken by conditioning them for loss through instigating acts of hatred towards each other. The spiritualist goes on to say to Genesis that someday your ancestors will reveal themselves to you and you will hear them and answer the call. The conversation is bringing some light to Genesis in her troublesome times then she asked the healer how will I know when this event will occur. The respond to Genesis question was by telling her that the moon cycle rules the night which the light reflects from the sun and within 24 hours is the greater influence balancing the planet. The electrical sun will phase out which is destroying the planet so, the magnetic Sun pulling by gravity connecting energy to enhance more pigmentation. Then when the force of the Suns energy accelerates it will reproduce you Genesis by strengthening the atoms. During the right season the temperature will continue to rise causing an explosion of solar flares from the Sun (Ra) returning the golden age and transforming you into a goddess. Substantially, the circuits within you will vibrate into an extraordinary absorption of power healing you Genesis causing you to become ageless as your body becomes a shield of armor. As carbon combines with other natural compounds you will metamorphose into a lucid genius and be capable of mind reading. Also, you will no longer need technology for communication a telepathic approach is the appropriate method to contact your ancestors for navigating to the stars. Astral traveling through meditation will become a common access of returning you to your family tree the ruling class of supreme authority. During absence Genesis from your African traditions and the indoctrination into the European world elders from Africa believe that the ancestral spirits has withdrawn from you. The spiritualist told Genesis that she was born with the gift of healing and magic and she would take Genesis through a long initiation process to reunite her body and soul. After the Ceremony Genesis disciplined herself for regular spiritual practices to transcend towards the path to salvation, liberation and a union with the ancestors. The spiritualist told Genesis during the golden age of Kemet, the black land of ancient people who existed was by a cultivation of the heat index witnessing creation. They honored their culture during extraterrestrial rule as they zoomed in on their sky boats with their knowledge of prophecy. During this period the temples were written in pyramid and coffin text (mdw n Tr) conveying every birth and death in detail, where the soul will go after departing from this life. The healer goes on to say that people from a divine bloodline must stop serving false gods and return to their former way of living then they will awake and remove the spell of kingu. A marginalized society evil forces will attempt to proceed against someone who has ultimate power. However, those who have pigment and shouldn't allow other groups to control their thoughts and actions. Although, the substance is classified by the amount of carbon in the pineal gland which is affiliated with an advanced intelligence and talent than other races of people. Blessing the dominant gene race with the capability to activate unseen and supernatural forces which seem to be suspended in a deep sleep due to the spell of kingu. Overall, the absence of carbon causes an undeveloped albino condition which is sensitive to the sun. Carbon is the key to life and the more someone has the more civil, intuition and information the brain can store. Therefore, an elevated dimension of sound and a wide range of light the eyes can absorb is the gateway to communicate with the ancestors. There are different types of the substances and Caucasian people have sulfur the lowest carbon content while black people have selenium the highest amount on the racial scale. However, biologically they're from a different trail of molecule but, the darker the more vitamin and minerals are in the bones. The African doctor explained to Genesis that you will illuminate many of your own people who are conformed against you. Those who impersonate and entertain brothers and sisters are down playing information to access power for themselves. Consequently, these nomads plan is to steal the aboriginal children divine source of power which is a combination of 9 ether and carbon by sexually or medically exchanging genes to infuse power. The justification for this act is to deceive the public into thinking that this defenseless and fractured class of people broke the law and must be annihilated. These individuals ordinarily are black women and children, the miss-educated, junkies, alcoholics, poor or vulnerable souls. Society are then miss-lead by the system tricking people into thinking that earth has no need for those who were spiritual. Only people who are willing to adapted to an indoctrinated belief of Lucifer which is under the protection of a temporary optical illusion. While the deception continues the children of the universal creator will continue consuming unhealthy foods and age from over exposure of manufactured radiation. These devices are extremely destructive on carbonated subjects which put out harmful radioactivty and kill the flesh. When allergic reactions attack body tissue bought on by chemicals used to preserve foods stopping the essence from where the seed yields. However, vegetation meals are less frequently indulged today but, hybrid foods are grown in laboratories and don't produce alkaline and electric properties to enhance the body duration. When foreign groups come to the U.S. they open their own grocery stores importing a food supply preserved with natural ingredients and no GMO's. Particularly, Africans, Indians from India, Arabs, Mexicans and some Latin and Asian groups you may need to sort through the rations. Overall, brothers and sisters need to invest into organic supermarkets or grow wholesome food themselves to live longer and healthier lives. Additionally, if the children of antiquity need medical attention they must seek care at a facility where doctors are educated in healing of those who have the dominant gene. Likewise, like our brother Dr. Sebi who taught that medicine for people of color are herb, root and bark combinations and aren't pharmaceutical drugs. Therefore, soon mother nature will replenish and savor the environment from the destruction of mankind then the nation can produce a wholesome harvest that is proper for sustaining good health. The African shaman continued to say apparently, the black race lost favor with the all mighty God and excepted a false concept of living after being deceived into thinking religion will guarantee their salvation. Many ebony sisters have characterized other races who led them to believe that they're unattractive because of misleading advertisements which neglects dark skin and a wooly hair people. Importantly, these sleeping goddesses have no idea of what true beauty is so, physiologically they suffer from dysphoria and deliberately relent to change themselves. They disregard that they immersed out of a mysterious queenly monarch before any other culture existed. Therefore, brothers and sisters won't have anything to do with black awareness just artificial and worthless materials that were inspired by capitalism. While they donate the dominate gene over to pigment deficient people in exchange for their recessive trait. Ignorantly, preserving a race who could care less about them or anything other than how to reproduce themselves and continue to attain power on the planet. These bandits are infamous for gaining wealth and by any means necessary as they dominate the entire world by trickery. Although, black people evolved from a divine source and can travel throughout realms because carbon is found in every perimeter in the universe. Instead the children of divinity fell from grace into an abomination on the 3D sphere and their DNA was altered using various animal for mutating mankind who now crave the flesh. Afterwards, the aboriginals were conditioned into thinking that the material world is a finale and when someone dies the spirit is inconclusive. However, these luxuries caused brothers and sisters to realize that they had been played in an exploited scheme to lose their soul. Hoping for acceptance from foreign groups who didn't receive them after they alienated they're own family tree. All the time the game was called socialism to other cultures gaining a fortune by hiring black people to work for their corporations. These black foolish graduates take their college degrees and go out of their community leaving it struggling to survive. Particularly, black celebrities, politicians, professional athletes and news anchors in this race based society where equal opportunity are for those who under contract. These selfish Blacks groups are the only race in America who exclude they're people because the stipulations of the guaranty exclude outsiders. Overall, foreigners who come to the U.S. don't associate themselves with others and are seldom seen socializing outside of their race. Black people are the only race who want to be excepted by others and it's for an opportunity to capitalize on their money. Then the average black class enjoyed seeing their people down because they don't understand how the game is played so, they remain under the spell of Kingu. The country is based on monopolizing the business arena and owning land and it is every race responsible to benefit from the commodity. Meanwhile, while brothers and sisters are fighting against one another every culture were controlling tangible resources and taken advantage of the U.S. partnership to earn wealth. Therefore, these manipulative and greedy people can get away with charging higher rates on mortgages, cars, hotel stays, receiving higher benefits, insurance ratio's and on all commodities which clearly indicates that equal rights are for other races. Although, African Americans still solely depend on other classes of people for raising and educating their children, housing, food and clothing. However, falling for the deception of religion, false advertising and refusing to believe that African history is not merit and the solution for better. While in privacy other groups capitalize from African studies and become influential in the world and sovereign while brothers and sisters are confined to servitude. Overall, Caucasians continue expressing their hatred against black people through murder, exhibits, movies, confederate flags, books, museums and at historical sites instigating a revolutionary war but, in a more sophisticated manner. Meanwhile, the indigenous ones over indulge in unhealthy food sold in fast food restaurants and Deli's across the nation leading to sickness and disadvantaged medical treatment. However, this kind of food don't support the DNA of black people causing a breakdown in health when the body lose the ability to perform tasks then other groups triumph. Then compensate for the loss black group by soliciting benefits from the government to maintain stability. Therefore, underhandedly these nomads were migrating to different regions around the globe characterizing the indigenous people from all over the world particularly Africa. Commonly, Africa is rich in natural resources so, invaders spoke the language, wore the garments, duplicated the recipes, mixed breed in every form of black culture to appear as if they have rights to the inheritance of the land there and abroad. Absolutely, don't bother to try negotiating with other groups in an agreement for better who genes are connected to the beast because of a calcified ancestry to animals. Someday, soon the educated brothers and sisters will awake and come to realize that they must leave the country before the all mighty remove the salvages from America and return the land to the true owners. Collectively, due to poor parenting it has devastated young black youth who are depending on the system to support unwanted babies out of weak and selfish motives. Otherwise, avoiding the responsibility of raising children and denying them what they deserve which is an opportunity to lead a productive life. The concept of getting free benefits has caused a destruction of the black civilization resulting in record numbers of future criminals and beggars. Now, these infidels have bought this idea to America with unlimited intentions to replace black people completely through genocide. However, other races are moving into the black community owning and operating businesses selling products that identify with African culture. Including: Caucasians, Asians, Arabs, Malaysians, American Indians, Indians from India, Alaskan Eskimos and some who also fell from favor among their tribe and became decisive on omitting black people out of the businesses world. However, when the temperature rise there will come a great demand for better bought on by the indigenous people who will decide to free themselves from the cage. Insisting that the only chance to succeed in business is that America individualize every foreign and domestic group allowing each of them to govern their own territory. Predominantly, resembling black wall street in Tulsa, Ok., during 1921 when African Americans independently industrialized their own communities. Owning banks, hotels, hospitals, cafes, movie theaters, real estate, clothing stores, supermarkets and indoor plumbing and a lot more. It was a time when Caucasians didn't have the same luxuries and black school teachers passed students with honors while whites were falling economically. Out of a hostile and racist mob of Caucasians attacked the wealthy black mecca looting, destroying homes and businesses by burning them down. Killing hundreds of brothers and sisters, children and left thousands homeless without a place to go. The African spiritualist goes on to explain to Genesis that for your people to restructure a deliberation of that analysis in correspondence to an enactment for change. Black people will then need to withdraw from this former administration that has held them back by boycotting and resisting businesses and the concept will bring enemies to its knees. Meanwhile, the shaman continued to say that the universe will charge an emerging flame of power into your atoms causing you to become a goddess Genesis allowing you crush every weapon known to man. During this time a small percent of black people will wake up soldiering in the resistance to accede spirituality and non-blacks you will not harm due to their efforts to help your people. This concept will continue in the 21st century when a few African Americans will rise in consciousness transiting into wisdom and break the spell of Kingu. As it was in ancient days when Ethiopia became a Coptic church and the daughter Kemet (Egypt) resolved the conflict but, was enslaved in battle for refusing to except another protocol. These are seeds of the ancient ones who tampered with the original plan of god and altered society. Therefore, the golden age is on the horizon when the temperature double causing non-carbonated people to migrate to low light areas before the sun blemished their skin to leper. Other pigment deficient people who choose to stay on earth's surface will take on a zombie affect. The blast of over exposure from the sun is destructive on albino's which doesn't recognize the hybrid. Reversing the present age into the former supreme ruling class of carbonated spiritual people who will govern. Due to the lack of resources and knowledge will put black people into a difficult position to maintain operation. Therefore, the ancestors will send an arriving African Calvary from the motherland in an act of support. Consequently, aboriginal people better hope that the Africans arrive and rescue remnants left from the aftermath and relocate them to areas of safety. However, the administration will be aware of the coming calamity as the timeline for ruler ship expires. Although, the native Indians who resided in the territory preserved the environment and connected with the universe in harmony and will be honored for their praise. Primarily, the land was invaded by salvages who used firearms to wipe out the inhabitants of the western hemisphere and claim the land for themselves. The action brought on by Caucasians was used to govern the territory has changed because the ancestors have had enough. The natives who occupied the region were peace keepers on the land and welcomed visitors. Although, it was forbidden to procreate outside of the tribe or you were removed from the lineage. The natives wept after they witnessed the land invaded then occupied by a murderous species who established rules and regulations for greed. Then enforced the concept through use of firearms as the strange beast arrived in ships coming in from the sea ending freedom in exchange for forced labor. Omitting the spiritual way of living by not honoring the planet then reconciled for material and religious beliefs which made America bad. The theory of control was impossible to love a false authority but, to worship meaninglessly and for a short-term worldly vision. The invading force promised goodwill for all people which contemplated nothing but, constant pain and suffering. In conclusion every individual had to fight for survival in order to prove that multi-racial interactions can work. Therefore, arguments addressing racism has never been solved when DNA corrupting remains paralyzed and the image of blackness are destroyed. Although, firearms were manufactured to protect salvages from Indians who already occupied the land causing so, much constant needless suffering. Under native inhabitancy weapons were used for hunting and to battle against other native tribes. Substantially, souls can reproduce than rather stay in hell amongst sodomite beast who believe that they have the right to control the planet. Meanwhile, the land will cleanse itself and re-connect to the continent of Africa the cradle of civilization the home of people of African descent. Genesis, Genesis the spiritualist spoke you have suffered a great deal of pain and misfortune but, you have endured like a champion. Predominantly, you are the sacrificial lamb who chosen for the task to set you people free making you the gatekeeper of harmony. Your mother was imparted concerning the ancient Kemet prophecy when you were a child and out of her sneaky little secret and her jealous rage she mistreated you. The losses and unhappiness that you endured will prepare you for change that will be an ultimate mind blowing episode. The shaman presented Genesis with a final surprise! you will not be alone, soon you will meet your kindred spirit your perfect match who will appreciate, defend and protect you. He will love you as you are and you will finally be happy and all the hell on earth that you have suffered maybe can be forgotten. Genesis weep happily after the African woman instructs her on how to channel into her powers because the time is inevitable and retribution is approaching. To activate your powers more affectively the spiritualist conveyed to Genesis and cultivate your strength is by purifying yourself at the bank of a river. Meditate three times a day in the morning when the sun is rising is Amen Ra, in the afternoon when the sun is high noon is Atum Ra, in the evening when the sun sets is Amon Ra. Give thanks to the all mighty creator and for all that you have been blessed with. Fast at times because the body can heal itself naturally then maintain an organic alkaline diet infused with chlorophyll and fresh fruits and vegetables with seeds. Don't eat packaged food unless it is preserved naturally, non-seeded foods are hybrid or food that is made of animal, human stock is filled with death and disease. These are foods which the body don't favor but, eat foods that are seasoned with natural herbs, spices, fruit, oil and vegetables. Fresh fruit and vegetables are rich in electric properties that the body recognize to enhance physical balance and restoration. People of African descent shouldn't consume foods injected with GMO's which cause a breakdown of the body and ruins health. Chemicals condition the body to adapt to pharmaceutical drugs, compounds used for long term treatment instead of herbs and roots for a cure. Primarily, African's who were brought to the U.S. and enslaved then forced to raise their children on left over scraps of meat from Massa's table and baby formula caused many unexplained sicknesses. Therefore, brothers and sisters must own and operate grocery stores importing foods from Africa and learn how to cook wholesome portions of meals. Foods made of beans and seasoned with curry or favorite spices adding dumplings, peas, potatoes for meat replacement and Fufu or Roti for dipping. Those who want food from the sea can try some palm nut adding dry fish, vegetable bullion, garlic, olive oil, tomato paste served over rice. Soups made of lentils and wholegrain breads with flaxseeds, sunflower, poppy seeds applying egg wash and cornmeal to the dough for a tasty and appealing affect. Plantains and Other vegetables can be cooked on low heat using coconut oil or power as a milk replacement. Veggies steamed close to raw seasoned with natural olive, almond, mango, coconut oil, adding spices for flavor and fresh seeded fruits with every meal. Aboriginal people who enjoy coffee and tea beverages can brew in cinnamon or grind some fresh hazelnut, clove, black pepper or nutmeg for chai. Instead of artificial spices that has no nutrition then eat plenty of walnuts, almonds, pecans or your favorite assortment. Moreover, sisters who are birthing babies should consider breast feeding verses baby formula because our DNA is different than other races. The breast milk of the black woman has more nutrients causing the baby to develop a lot faster than any other group. However, ingredients which are found in baby formula is human based from other races and some found in purified cow's milk so, they should use caution when feeding their baby. Therefore, hospitals don't have groups who are educated and qualified to heal patients who has black DNA and they already know that many African Americans become sick through food consumption of GMO'S. Therefore, when African Americans awaken into their new life of herbs, barks and root combinations for the cure of every disease that is known to man. Sisters who have heavy bleeding and fibroids due to tension and stress can take the herb Pau' De Arco to decrease the bleeding and shrink the cyst. Those who are diagnosed with cancer or have tumors can take combinations of herbs, roots and barks to kill the cancer and shrink the tumor. Garlic, cayenne pepper, milk thistle, turmeric, bloodroot, fever few, wheat grass, butchers broom, sheep's sorrel, astragalus or you can purchase flora essence of these blends. Vitamin E or fish oil is common for preventing heart attacks caused by eating unhealthy fat which stop the blood flow to the heart and cinnamon keeps the blood pressure balanced. Those who suffer from various skin conditions should use essential oil in the bath, dead sea salt for a spa and wash with organic soap. Then apply African shea butter to the skin for moisturizing which is grown in west and central Africa and is harvested from trees. Pharmaceuticals are manufactured in Laboratories which are for treating patients long term and doctors rely on marketing the drug to accumulate big profits verses herbal remedies for a cure. It was phenomenal what the healer express to Genesis and out of curiosity she purchased a microscope from a local business who sales medical equipment to examine her blood type at home. In the privacy of her experiment Genesis discovered that the color in her gene resembled patterns of primordial light. The design was traced from cosmic activity throughout space exposing that she has the same DNA make-up of the Gods. After Genesis learned that her gene matched every compound in the universe and she couldn't be immunized because she had the same bloodline of ancient deities. Genesis continued testing DNA samples and noticed that the results showed that the dominant gene became an abomination which was corrupted by mix breeding of various animals. The test results also made Genesis aware that carbon is a blessed substance which can reproduce itself and return to a form of divine energy. This gift can become immortal like a seed that continues to return and never die but, the recessive gene showed no capacity to procreate. Therefore, many Atheist don't believe that deities control the universe and in conclusion insist that people are beings of matter and are floating about as energy. Although, the trait of a recessive gene is connected to wild beast of a different gender or species. However, scientifically a physical object can't exist in the universe that don't express color because the reproductive organisms won't sustain DNA. Overall, the universe is compatible with the dominant gene and recognize the genealogy of carbon tracing to the aboriginal being. Substantially, the people of antiquity were here before and some of them are the former prophets who came back to re-establish a reunion on earth. Meanwhile, Genesis tested the recessive gene it traced the European group called the RH-FACTOR which means RHESUS short for RHESUS "MONKEY". RH-POSITIVE is a substance antigen which stimulate the animal body from agglutinin an anti-body. The protein is found in the blood stream of a Rhesus monkey who origin is traced in North America, Asia and Central Africa. Discovered to be a hybrid structure which is a different gender of another species and clearly the genealogy of the Caucasian race. Scientifically, proves that RH- FACTOR is not a product of mix-breeding but, a result of an evolutionary monkey source. Genesis questioned herself about when did other species arrive on the scene but, couldn't find a date. Although scientist used DNA as evidence that they evolved differently while the behavior and way of life were unlike the dominant people. Therefore, black parents need to stop passing on what they were conditioned to believe to their offspring. Because substantially, the children will reap the harvest of what their parent have done and that generation will be against them. Otherwise, Africans are naturally RH-NEGATIVE and should never allow RH-POSITIVE blood to enter their blood stream because the blood will develop red-blood hemolysis (blood protein) causing a break down. RH-NEGATIVE African's came from the Nephilim that was cast down and fell short of glory and have super human strength. The Nephilim are the sons of god or the watchers and the RH-NEGATIVE blood meaning they belong to the extraterrestrial bloodline who are the children of the sky father and earth mother. Genesis also, discovered that in Sumer the alien race of Gods was known as the Anunnaki who occupied another planet in the solar system called Sirius by the Sumerians. Anu was the captain of the mothership (Sirius) called the twelfth planet which was home of advanced technology. The twelve planets are the Sun, Mercury, Venus, Earth, Luna, and Mars within the asteroid belt then you have Jupiter, Saturn, Uranius, Neptune, Pluto and Sirius (Nibiru) which is outside of the asteroid belt when pirates invaded the planet. However, when the Anunnaki, a group of deities who landed in Mesopotamia colonizing it and altered black DNA by mating with humans creating Demigods or men of renown, (Genesis 6:4) Enki and Enlil as one-half of Adam and the other Neanderthal making creation ¼ less black. Demonstrating that the combination of the two genes has clear evidence of who is the greater (god) and who is the lesser (enemy). The African spiritualist insisted that mix-breeding is leading to a state of genocide because the universal creator didn't create a mix race, kinsmen did. The people of antiquity was warned in the written word not to have anything to do with other races because these children will begin to follow their practices. The beliefs of this species didn't know god and introduced a demonic culture to the children of god who followed them relying on a material foundation to live by. Numbers 25:1-3 and Leviticus 19:19, Deuteronomy 7:3-4 You shall not intermarry with them because they will turn your sons away from following me, acts 15:24, Exodus 34:10-16 God opposed interracial marriage, Rev. 21:27, Proverb 11:1. Therefore, these beings are of a different stock and think, act, walk, talk, move, differently and their rhythm and tones are unlike the dominant gene. Out of an astonishing surprise the recessive gene sample had a calcified affect which caused a salvage behavior and was dead with very low senses not capable of 360 degree of knowledge. However, a God has carbon and 9 Ether (wooly hair) in the gene to be recognized by nature and all along this was the stigma that martyred the black holocaust against black people. Substantially, the dominate gene beings robed themselves of their pigment through mix breeding and became pale (Seth) the lowest part of who they were. All around the 1940's this species began a study of human cells for creating a hallow graphic world (disguise) to continue the deception of an artificial intelligence. Throughout, a study Genesis found out that the dominant gene can duplicate ancient deities by raising the spiritual center. Altogether, the offspring of dark matter up in the cosmos where the ancestors live are a group of carbonated warriors who continued to reincarnate on earth to solve the injustice. Overall, Genesis had to face the reality that the U.S. was founded on genocide for the intent of greed by force of military while robing Africa of her rich natural resources. The entire concept bewitched Genesis when the high cost of living in America was leading to astronomical loss of businesses, jobs and cut backs. Likewise, during the 1930's a decision made world war 11 which seemed to be the only hope to gain momentum in the U.S. Meanwhile, Genesis found out that Amen Ra was already inside of her and out of that power she can raise to a high level of a deity. Also, how to recolonize to the advanced star system using the spirit to navigate the soul towards home from the gateway of the pyramids. However, the data Genesis received from the experiment supported the results when she used a telescope to visualize the evidence in the universe. Meaning that black people can manifest into many form of life and in many realms beyond this civilization. After Genesis found out that she was the offspring of the gods she became determine to seek how this change will manifest so, she traveled to the forest to be near nature.

Genesis visits Florida the deep south chapter 9

Genesis purchased a map to use for a compass to determine the next direction that she would travel after positioning her finger on the blueprint, it settled on the city of Tampa, Fl. However, Genesis found her way to the ocean shore on the gulf to get through the bitterly cold winter in New York city. There Genesis focused on the predictions that the African shaman told her often wondering if answering the call was truly a destined course of events. Then she cleansed herself by a river bank as the healer told her and took long walks through the forest. The temperature was nearly 85 degrees with beautiful beaches everywhere and she enjoyed it but, a lot of people that Genesis encountered were immoral. They were preoccupied with using and pushing dope in the drug trafficking wonderland making it implement to build the tropical state. Prostitution was common and gentlemen clubs were all over the place beseeching all day booty shaking risking catching a disease just to earn a few dollars. Churches were plentiful but, members harassed Genesis all the time trying to solicit information about her beliefs because they couldn't explain their own biblical theory. Genesis met black Floridians who thought that Muslim's were the enemy and Christian the savior proceeding to attack her. The entire atmosphere in the sunshine state was filled with hopeless energy of a lost generation of 75 % black people. Later, Genesis found a record of data at a radio station showing a huge number of rapist and people who were infected with the HIV virus stalking innocent people for sexual favors and financial advances. Now, coming from the east coast Genesis wasn't use to the open aggressiveness and fornicating obscenity which was unacceptable for the young woman. Men from the big city had a more appropriate approach they asked a woman out then got to know the family and friends. Racism in Florida was unbelievable and Genesis thought that it was still during the times of Jim Crow when Caucasians was barbaric and belligerent with their behavior. Genesis was called the word nigger over 15 times by drive by rednecks and Spanish people who were screaming Negros out of passing vehicles. Some foreigners would pretend to be hip just to capitalize on brothers and sisters expressing concerns on how black people use slavery as an excuse to fail. Lots of men used foolish and pathologically damaged women to work full time jobs while they stay home sleeping all day and up walking at night selling dope. These races were hiding out in black low-income communities trying to prevent their people from knowing that they were losers. Indians from India was pouring in to Florida from one of the poorest countries in the world assuming black people were lazy operating rundown filthy motel establishments. Asians were quietly keeping their thoughts to themselves afraid of the day when the aboriginal people will wake up and embrace their African roots. Then reign again as Kings and Queens ruling as a superior class of beings. Although, the yellow race worshiped a counterfeit over weight Buddha and can no longer take advantage of black people ignorance. However, everywhere Genesis stayed was invaded by European landlords once they observed her conscious wear and felt threatened by her intelligence. Meanwhile, the entire state of Florida was crawling with rednecks and crackheads who landlords rented apartments to black people after this group destroyed units. The occupied spaces were backed up with feces in tubs, kitchen sinks and toilets then expect tenants to clean it after moving in. Then the slum lords threaten eviction even after renting under condemned conditions that they better not complain. These people were nasty and frightened by aboriginal people who will eventually tap into their metaphysical power but, for the moment was still under the spell of kingu. Therefore, Black people were still being charged more for rent than other groups while they used the money to give their people affordable rates. Separating blacks from the better portion of units and their people in the newly renovated sections. A few black realtors fell into the same pattern of renting rundown sections to their own people and better units to other races. Then hire sorry brothers who express feelings of self-hatred towards themselves and argue against black people if they complain but, roll out the red carpet for other races. Whereas, black people insist on going all out to take care of other groups before their own but, when the situation is reversed they don't get the same courtesy. Therefore, most black people expression of each other is awful so, don't even bother to go into business with them because they might show up more than 4 hours late or if at all. Generally, a brother or sister working independently should have a good reputation of how they do business or check out their reviews. Overall, the explanation they give you is nothing but excuses but, when dealing with Caucasian people they're always on time to say yes Massa. However, if that brother or sister is successful then they come running back begging for the opportunity to work with them. Altogether, many super markets and restaurants were poisoning black folk food and immediately after eating your running to the bathroom with irritable bowel syndrome, a virus or breakout. Businesses would serve Caucasians before black people angering Genesis to resist by going without what she didn't need. In today's time Genesis refused to believe that a multi-racial society can work because of cultural differences. Later, Genesis was asked several times to remove her hijab when entering a room because other groups assumed that she was a terrorist. Although, the covering represented obedience to the creator, righteousness, protection, faith, dignity and honor. Altogether, people in America were intimidated if a black person appeared to be conscious or educated concerning their African heritage. These indigenous ones are blessed who cherish their culture and uphold a unique presence in the world by wearing conscious designed attire. Therefore, Genesis wore her garment it put her in an awkward situation with sisters who felt animosity because they weren't ready for an uprising that would carry them to freedom. Genesis was amongst the few in her race who didn't allow the lack of knowing her roots to divide and conquer the village. Most of the aboriginal people had been conditioned for so, long by the system even family made it difficult to cope with their own people and embrace African culture. Sisters and brothers hated Genesis for being different and they couldn't relate to her although she showed them love and support but, they deceived her making her suffer. When Genesis visited various cities in Florida she discovered that people lived backward and Caucasians were extremely racist. There were all day beggars and homeless people who were delusional by demanding that strangers take care of them. The hospitals and police department was malicious considering horrifying stories Genesis heard. Black people were going into the hospital for a minor aliment and coming out of with their health ruined and unnecessary limbs and organs were stolen. Another frighten story was about a black female who was admitted into Tampa General Hospital, handcuffed to the bed and shot in the chest by a Caucasian deputy because she asked for the light to be off at night so, she could sleep better. The patient was then released without medical attention and forcefully removed from the facility by a black security officer which still shows how a house nigger is used against the field nigger. A ratio determined how medical facilities were giving excellent care to Caucasian people while black people health was deliberately destroyed. Genesis was convinced that a continuous act of racism was being committed against black people but, in a sophisticated and deceiving manner. Proving that black people are perpetually dehumanized by Caucasians and other groups also, treated them like second class citizens. Genesis passed through Hillsborough county which has some of the most racist Caucasian police officers in the country who stereo-type young black youth as criminals because of the color of their skin. The reason for the stigma against them was to shoot them down in cold blood without identifying themselves and penalty for an offense. Many Ku Klux Klan were hiding behind police uniforms, doctors, lawyers, and judges title to clear themselves of their mischievous conduct against people of color. Then use the system to falsely arrest brothers and sisters who have no money, power or support in a plan for their defense to sabotage the record. Local newspapers and news stations simply avoided reporting criminal acts against black people in Florida to hide the fact that racism in the deep south haven't ended. Although, there is not a chance for justice while Caucasians rule and no matter how much evidence blacks has proving their innocence that dark skin will always find cause. In March of 1857 a Dred Scott case for freedom ended in a ruled decision that black people have no rights and wasn't American citizens and was never considered to honor by chief justice Roger Taney. That ruling is still expressed today causing Caucasians to feel that they have the right to continue murdering innocent black people and get away with it. The salvage beast get away with it because brothers and sisters are afraid to fight and stand-up for what is right making it an uncomfortable place to live. However, every race that was wronged by the Caucasian group received reparations except for black people. Although, if black people love one another then they reclaim their heritage, customs and way of life. Meanwhile, the beast had persuaded other groups to also, manipulate brothers and sisters for additional power and control. The entire globe was in on the game to take control of the Africa's rich natural resources because black people were afraid to fight for their homeland and themselves. Since the Atlantic slave trade African Americans have been victimized on Florida plantations and for so, long that they are still feeling the sting of the slave owners whip. Therefore, the salvage beast continued flying confederate flags from passing vehicles and monuments across the state. Overall, black people thought that the only solution they had left was to play out uncle tom roles. Then they integrated and breed with the offspring of their former slave master's children and lived with the comfortable lie. Deliberately destroying the African kabbalah rooted out of the constellation of stars (civilizations) where the plan of returning the spirit to the womb was dead. The disconnection caused the spiritual center of the aboriginal ones to suspend itself when the ability to recognize the pro-type of god was loss and can no longer access divinity. Meanwhile, brothers and sisters were renting cabins in Florida that resembled slave quarters during the arrival of the slave ships. When African slaves received a written version of the bible based on Jesus after the Anunnaki had already left the tablets of life with Adapa (Adam). Whereas, the Florida gulf is blessed with sunshine all year but, the children of the sun turned into vampires who come out at night because they didn't know Ra. Largely, they were taught by Europeans not to except supreme light energy that give life throughout the universe since it's destructive on the body. These dead souls are beggars, asking people their business, applying for benefits, on the run criminals and chasing innocent people to infect with the HIV virus. In fear of rednecks (Massa) in the deep south is primarily why the black man get beat up and his children killed. However, the foolish black race was taught to wait on a savior who will come along and settle the score instead of awaken the warrior spirit and battle it out. Therefore, there is no way a Caucasian man can beat up an African warrior unless it in the movies or he is pumped up on steroids. Even though Caucasians only interest in integrating with black people is capitalism and to preserve their recessive seed. A record number of men were neglecting the family role of responsibility to engage into a losing status of homosexuality. It's common in Florida for weak worthless men to send foolish women off to a full work week preventing any possibility of welcoming family and friends. Living like a hermit in a paranoid state of fear because they are afraid to engage in social functions and mingle with people. While the losers become comfortable on a level of insanity which waits like a bomb ready to explode. Genesis was very familiar with a dysfunctional atmosphere when growing up and experienced a tremendous number of loved ones fall in a pattern of eccentric conduct. In regards to Genesis raising a family of her own it began to look less likely for any chance of having children. Genesis looked at the concept of family as contagious for the next generation who were ignorant of the spell of Kingu. Causing the energy to reverse into a temporary life which ends in aging, suffering and death by an un-natural way of living. Therefore, aboriginals need to remove themselves from GMO's, manufactured devices and chemicals that prevent the supernatural realm to manifest and make them sick. Including food, appliances, cell phones, computers, television, cars, florescent lighting, black shades that block sun light, and everything that doesn't please nature. Then they can access magical power and strength by an unseen ability through meditation an adrenaline stimulation. Meanwhile, the children of nuance were ruining their health by applying skin lightening cream onto their skin. Now, the ingredients in the ointment were chemical based and has been a determined medical factor for skin disease. It was Just another device used to prevent brothers and sisters from becoming awakening gods and goddesses. It's a scientific fact that people of color are weakened when out of touch with the wild which is their natural habitat and can access a magnificent source of power. An example of this proven theory was when black people stole from each other, destroyed, and prevented each other from progressing is an unbalanced factor causing their frequency to operate on low. Brother against brother and sister against sister has robed the village of the fruit and the result is a false concept of reality. The Atlantic slave trade was the complexed connecting component needed by Caucasians for black people to become fearless and no longer the conquering warriors of antiquity. Meanwhile, Genesis envisioned a season when the anointed brothers and sisters would wake-up and return to their original origin in Africa. After removing themselves from the source that's been holding them back and they can be more loving towards each other and productive within their own environment. Although, throughout the 21st century integration failed in America but, it benefited others groups who are still capitalizing on black people and the system. The concept caused loss and trust in each group with consequences which were devastating ending in a hopeless catastrophe of casualties. Brothers and sister accomplished goals at a higher degree when they were separated from other races. However, Genesis was in Florida for the winter waiting for the moment to return to east coast when suddenly she was involved in a hit and run car accident by a driver who was texting on the phone. The vehicle spun around repeatedly bashing her head against the wind shield after she was whacked by the driver. The person driving left her medically confined to therapy suffering with severe pain and torn ligaments. Genesis thought that she was finished because she lost the vehicle and couldn't walk anymore to sell her products that she depended on to pay bills. Afterwards, some male strangers showed up periodically and rescued her but, they weren't sincere just opportunist who were looking for sex. When Genesis refused the proposition out of disappointment they waited to watch her struggle into a frightening and perilous surge. Primarily, people that she befriended deserted her in a major time of need looking on without conviction, monitoring Genesis healing process while deviously waiting to see her fall. Fortunately, the forces of the ancestors moved in Genesis favor when they heard her grievous call and helped her survive the incident proving that she wasn't forgotten. The accident opened a gateway for Genesis realizing that it was time for the aboriginal people to wake-up or perish. It was during a time when brothers and sisters were facing massive killings by racist police, drugs, injustice, sickness and disease was at astronomical high. False imprisonments were in place, drugs were breaking up families and communities, destroying good health then Genesis thought about a fly which land on everything that is filthy became the essence of people. Many hated they're pigment but, they were lost and divided, some would turn on you because they didn't work towards a rewarding outcome within the race and they should be closely watched. Others just sold out to the beast participating in their celebrations that target aboriginal people and no other groups for deception. The celebrations don't identify with African culture at all and another portion was afraid to fight the strong the forces that were against Gods people. Besides, the sell outs were calling the police on brothers and sisters who were keeping it real so, Genesis insisted that it was time for a change. Then Genesis waited patiently while she yearned to see her call unfold that the female African spiritualist prophesied. One day while Genesis was spending time with nature a deep voice appeared speaking to her. Genesis answered, yes in another encounter with an ancestor who informed her that there will be great troubles coming to America. During Genesis conversation with God she was told not to enter New York city because an enormous earthquake will hit the metropolis city destroying major ports crippling the United States. Temperatures will rise beyond 150 degrees bringing about the return of a golden age where people of color can live in harmony again. Giving them the opportunity take back possession of the land and because of carbon and 9 Ether they have an ability to withstand up to 1250 degrees of Fahrenheit. Out of envy of the indigenous people reclaiming the land will cause resentment by Caucasian people and a genocide of corpse stock pile. Harp technology will be used cool the temperature to a comfortable and satisfying degree where people who lack color can survive on the planet. Otherwise, the engineering method of Harp can cause an imbalance in nature when seasons were out of order creating terrible hurricanes, tornados, floods, earthquakes and other acts by mother nature. Unexpectedly, Harp technology will malfunction raising temperatures to soar while other groups turned to the indigenous people for forgiveness. Therefore, pushing pigment deficient people into an underground abyss cutting them off from resources giving brothers and sisters ruler ship status. Catastrophically, lifestyle and business will struggle miserably because of no import connections for goods. Later, an African Calvary will show up to help get brothers and sisters recover from the calamity given them resources needed to get the country back in order. Meanwhile, food crop will spoil causing cannibalism and the recessive gene beings who stayed above ground will hibernated into sodomites developing tails exposing their true nature. Then trees and grass from one end of the country burns by the hands of these salvages who will destroy many properties and livestock causing contamination on the surface of earth. Oceans will lift tides of dangerous poisons causing thousands of dead fish to float to shore and tap water become unhealthy to consume killing many and people. Therefore, an abyss will open on the earth which is reserved for wicked souls to go who disrespected the ancestors land and without no escape. These shameful souls are disconnected from glory and the opportunity to restore their souls literately are disbarred. Air planes will be snatched from the sky while the enemy of god try to orbit a getaway plan from the ruins but, a gravitational current will pull them out of compass. America is going up in smoke and become over populated with scary humanized demons who will hid themselves behind holograms in position to take over earth. Then the material world should have been inhabited by spiritual beings who have knowledge of architecture and build a foundation suited for a righteous way of living. However, the soulless one came to earth building without equipment and deceived many into thinking the structure would be of benefit to those of a lesser god. Meanwhile, after integration was declared law and the concept of a multi-racial foundation would work led to another set-back for African Americans to go nowhere. Before integration African Americans had knowledge of business so, Caucasians were surprised when they accepted a system believing in equal and fair rights. Then after the brutal attacks that the black nation suffered at the hands of the beast brought on crucial times and plagued a new generation of black people. Therefore, when elders led their children to rely on other classes of people to control their capital created a major setback. Instead of passing down sovereignty a determining factor for success meaning to own real estate and businesses in the community to maintain a fair share of commonwealth. However, stop the dependency on other groups who take advantage of the situation by charging higher prices for housing and drive black people out of their homes. Likewise, black people also, they pay higher food cost in their community than others, for clothing, vehicles, insurance and other needs which are causing a big loss of everything worked for. Then huge corporations trick customers in spending on cards to take their money and leave a frustrating trail to re-credit the account when service went bad. Likewise, African ancient deities created other races through a grafted process in a chronological order of events. Therefore, generated an existence of strange species making African people the mother and father of the world. Overall, brothers and sisters should be treated with honor and respect but, instead discredited with envy and jealousy. Unfortunately, African American parents have taught their children to rely on another group who has conditioned them to finance their own oppression. By spending every penny in their community with businesses overrun by foreigners and less than 1 percent to exchange with their own people. Meanwhile, Genesis took a survey on why her people were falling economically and discovered that foreigners were sharing expenses in the home to send children off to college or help towards purchasing real estate. However, when foreigners arrived to America they are more loving towards each other so, they invest their money into family businesses. Black people have been Americanized and taught not to trust each other and to do things single handedly stressing themselves out causing all kinds of health problems. Therefore, the stigma with black people is that they think the game is about being in competition with one another while with other groups insist the tournament is against outsiders. Sadly, aboriginal people are caught up in a jungle honoring the beast instead of against the beast while wealthy people who reside in high places are entertained by the foolishness. Moreover, in fear of the cage the indigenous ones drown themselves in drunkenness, homosexuality, rape, drugs, prostitution, theft, the comfort of lies, murder and all kind of ungodliness. However, everywhere Genesis went she met with black people all over the country but, particularly in Florida who refused to believe that African studies were the solution to their problems. They continued to resent being of African descent hating their black skin and depending solely on Caucasians for a better life. Although, African American parents privately discuss racism but, follow false leadership who suggest that when their children become eighteen years old kick them out of the house. Then achieve success themselves which is certainly not an African custom and without any capital to maintain an apartment or car and a maybe an extended family. The concept of this idea has ending in record numbers of black youth becoming homeless due to the impossible task. Although, these parents take pharmaceuticals recommended by doctors who are in the business of greed filing medical records of an incorrect diagnosis. Therefore, patients are unaware of what is wrong with them while trusting doctors who are chasing money by prescribing drugs they don't need causing schizophrenia and then parents ability to think logically is gone. However, the miss-conception has ended in recklessness, homelessness, begging on the street and a multitude of black folk who have left the village. Generations ago the indigenous ones addressed issues in the community by a meeting and not an individual who formed an opinion. Meanwhile, lots of black people were getting sick and some dying from eating chemically preserved foods and thought a cure was by using prescription drugs rather than herbal remedies. Then religious freaks come up with a solution that waiting for Jesus is the answer for all problems when black people have reproductive cells that will return into an egg. The prototype of a creator who blessed them with instructions already inside of them who can channel supernatural energy when they discover the method. The technique was by activating seven souls of Ra (Sefech Ba Ra) which is the highest dimension of life force energy that connects to all. This power is inside the children of God which is their plan of salvation but, instead they believe false teachings taught in the high council of synagogues of satanic cults throughout the world. Someday, the sons and daughters of god will resist the demonic forces of Lucifer and bring about change for better. Therefore, the children of God are the saviors or High Priest and can correct the problem already. The trouble that has been plaguing black people since allowing others to govern their fate by enforcing they're false agenda. Meanwhile, a decision will be made to boycott businesses that are overrun by other classes of people merchandise which is overpriced and don't do business with other groups. Then brothers and sister can take control of their own money and create an atmosphere that is more suitable for their community. However, it's not common sense and ignorant to choose to impress other groups by proving that the one can make the over price payment. Generally, beware of the house nigger who are in disguise by looking like you and giving the impression of consciousness but, has conspired against you. Genesis began to noticed that a lot of black people were hired and put in prestigious positions to appear integrated to save the region from retribution. Overall, the enslavement of the children of the all mighty god was to remove this species from the planet for the demonic actions against the indigenous ones who still were looked upon as niggas by the salvages. Although, Caucasians are under the protection of their own demonic and negative forces who was also, willing to safeguard these house niggers trying to avoid the responsibility of reparations owed to African Americans. This concept bought about a gateway of weak and worthless men who no longer wanted the responsibility of family because they became Americanized taking on the habits of the beast. Therefore, the children of antiquity can't love god and serve the ways of mankind eating animal meat as a delicatessen which turn one into salvages. Otherwise, consume vegetarian foods for a divine connection to the creator, celebrate life with family and friends, burn incense and meditate to activate chakra's (Sefech Ba Ra) but, most choose to chase the material world which has replaced a loving existence. These actions Led to mental illness, a homosexual path or some tattoo freak that are raising children into total confusion. These unfortunate actions are causing women to go without the support of a male figure feeling the only alternative for happiness is to become a lesbian too. The children of god are encouraged to work for Lucifer excepting jobs in the medical field that don't support black DNA but, the focus is on a treatment for a recessive gene. Overall, taking jobs that allow brothers and sister to imitate the salvage beast while destroying their own people, degrading themselves to keep their jobs when they should have been working for themselves all along. Matthew 4:8 teaches that the Messiah was offered the whole world that was set-up by satanic forces which wasn't his to give anyway. This concept has angered the holy creator because one can't live in the ways of the beast and honor god so, these children will not return to the family tree. Meanwhile, as the golden age arrives color deficient people will start to feel an affect of the sun ray's attacking their body by eating at the flesh while their eyes drip in blood by raising savage impulses. This event will take the world by storm because sodomy is considered a criminal act in many countries when a man and women sexual behavior are exhibited by anal, oral or engaging in sex with animals. Therefore, the universe refuse to tolerate ungodliness while the wild beast was out to devour the righteous and catch like prey. However, the ancestors gave Genesis a revelation that earth will soon be restored during the reshaping of events and it will be at the end of a black man presidential term. Then Genesis returned to New York again to warn friends of the impending danger before the time of the disaster expires. Before Genesis returned to the big city she decided to go to Los Angeles again to shop traveling by Amtrak and she observed beautiful valleys which surrounded the fun city. Then within the boundaries was a homeless crisis that was a lot worse than her first encounter as Christianity invaded the scene and men had no respect for a woman. Altogether, a brother had lost respect for the black Madonna after exposing his penis during sitting in a parked vehicle smoking crack and watching pornography. Long streets of businesses were closed due to the sluggish economy and many brothers had become house niggers and was hooked on Jesus energy. The brother's masculinity felt threatened by Genesis ability to move product in struggling times and called security to have her removed at Superior supermarket on Crenshaw and Imperial. The same misfortune struck Leimert park in Los Angeles, Ca which is primarily occupied by black people and looked like a ghost town filled with abandon units. Although, locals thought the problem could be solved politically by petitioning voters instead of money so, Genesis was fed up and went to New York.

Genesis meets her kindred spirit

Chapter 10

After Genesis warned her friends back home concerning the coming distress on New York City strangely, she decided to return to Florida. After set-backs she encountered earlier in the gulf state and wasn't sure of what direction to take form there. Everything Genesis did ended in disaster while she was alone for many years learning how to be good company to herself. Although, at times she Genesis longing for a committed friendship that could be shared with someone of similar interest. Unfortunately, Florida was the unlikely place to consider a friend because the region was running rampant with religious freaks harassing people about lord and savior issues. Overall, it was just a bunch of Europeanized black people who treated their own people like second class citizens after abandoning their culture. When there wasn't any concrete evidence to back up the crazed dilemma of a religion being the sure salvation to impede on innocent souls. Genesis realized that she was already in hell and often wondered what did she do to get there when people are rewarded for doing wrong and others suffer for doing what is right. However, society was continuing to struggle with racism which had no ending in sight because every race was on some power and control trip. Whereas, history teach you that dominant gene beings ruled spirituality and what goes around come around. Genesis was in badly need of a break after rising from many set-backs so, she decided to rent a hotel room with a pool to relax as evening approached. Anyway, she took a brief walk around the property in the cool of night to get a feel of where she was. Generally, she took a brief glance into the office window and there she viewed the most charming looking brown skinned man. Genesis felt chemistry and a unique presence coming from the brother as if he was a soul connected to divinity. However, Genesis never met another man who she loved and trusted since the loss of Ian and it was many years after she fell in love again. This brother was different from other men that she met throughout her travels he wasn't ordinary, he had a warrior spirit, tall with a pleasant looking demeanor. After fantasizing about the handsome cinnamon complexioned brother Genesis entered her room thinking no more about him. Another day he knocked on her door and introduce himself, hi, I am a manager at the hotel and my name is Indigo. I want to acquaint myself with you because I have instructed my maids to only clean your room when you are here. Genesis asked him, why would you do that and he answered saying that you have a lot of things that can get missing. Then Genesis responded, thank you and he went away and she remained curious about Indigo's concern for her belongings. The next day Genesis went out to sell products and she met a mature passing female who mentioned that her husband was in town giving Genesis a strange feeling. Then another day Genesis was hanging around the hotel and watching quest enjoy the pool while on her way to the front desk Indigo noticed Genesis form a distance. He was taking by her beauty and he began to follow her and accidently bumped into the young woman to initiate a casual conversation. Indigo wanted Genesis bad but, he was confused and didn't know how to approach the enchanting young woman of that caliber and didn't want to blow it. Generally, Indigo came to work every day waiting for a glimpse at Genesis and every moment he saw her his heart beat briskly and he fantasized about a love affair with her. Indigo was also, a real estate developer with a background in accounting and has family who respect his decisions and never challenged him. When Indigo saw Genesis the next day after glancing into her luminous eyes she released a spell that held him in captivity. Genesis radiant energy was so intense that Indigo could tap into the magical mystery that was inside of her which led to they're pre-destined encounter. However, Indigo didn't allow others to control his happiness so, he was perfect for Genesis. Likewise, Genesis didn't allow anyone to violate her authority and if they did they were removed from her threshold. Throughout, Genesis stay at the hotel handsome Indigo continued starring at her and conjuring up conversations when she passed by but, all the hurt she endured from the past just over took her. Genesis kept her guard up to prevent infringing on Indigo with bias trials and tribulations she had to undergo earlier. Primarily, Genesis wanted to resolve the duration of hardships from her past but, the hope of better never came. Genesis felt Indigo's affection and she loved him too but, she needed more time to sort out her imperfections which seemed to be haunting her. Furthermore, Genesis knew that Indigo was special and deserved respect so, she called on the spirit of the ancestors to protect him from unrighteous souls who was out to destroy honorary people. Genesis felt like she was under a curse and was afraid to tell Indigo that family abandoned her because he may not want a woman who didn't have roots. Later, Genesis found an apartment in Florida and stayed for a short time because her heart was home in New York. Therefore, she decided to return to the big city in denial of loving Indigo who sincerely and deeply cared for her in his soul. When Genesis arrived in New York she continued to sell her products door to door and her clients were happy to see her again. Shortly, after arriving home Genesis was selling her products in East Orange and Newark, New Jersey and she met a sister preaching on the street. The woman startling stops her to say that the spirit spoke to her about a marriage to someone who she recently loved. Genesis laughs and responded to the stranger there is no one in my life but, the preaching woman insisted that there is special man who is the match and he is missing you. This man is the one for you and you must return to him then Genesis replies "he is the one" are you insane I can only take so much. I just left Florida and there was someone I met who was interesting and I am frustrated with bull but, the preaching woman still insisted. On another day in Crown Heights, Brooklyn Genesis goes into a barber shop to sell her products and a stranger from the Caribbean island mentioned that she was about to get married and described the man. Moreover, not again Genesis thought to herself this is incredible who are you people and why do you keep telling me about a marriage. Everywhere, Genesis went strangers continued to tell her the same thing day after day and she decided to test her fate to find out the meaning. Genesis did love Indigo and returned to Florida but, when she got to the hotel Indigo was no longer working there and in frantic she asked about him but, got no answers. Anyway, Genesis decided to stay in the area to find out if the meaning of the saying since she felt right about Indigo. Then Genesis continued to sell her products door to door thinking if it's meant to be I'll find Indigo. Afterwards, she was caught off guard by some drive by stranger who insisted that she is bringing hope to the people but, it felt more like a setback on herself. Genesis was a street hustler who traveled frequently and knew how to make money to house herself during a weak economy. Overall, Floridian's became familiar with

Genesis method to move product so, she was the tidal wave of money making ideas for brothers and sisters in the community. Although, brothers and sisters insisted on expressing views that Genesis has a calling on her life when she could barely pay rent. Then locals attempted to apply Genesis principals for making money independently and the reality was disappointing after they discovered it takes a special gift to bring in capital. Out of envy they begin spreading nasty rumors and fabricated malicious gossip creating an uncomfortable atmosphere for Genesis. Whereas, Genesis knew that she had to find her man and get the hell out of Florida after feeling those negative vibrations advancing towards her. Another occasion Genesis was confronted again by a sister that she met frequently in a business concerning the handsome man who mysteriously disappeared. Considerably, a lot of time had gone by and the tale of the handsome man seemed to be fading away and Genesis was concerned that a reunion wouldn't materialize. Unexpectedly, one day when Genesis was about to give up on finding Indigo while she was walking along the street he drove up in a vehicle and they embraced. In fear of losing Genesis Indigo explained that he was in love with her from the first time he saw her. Mainly, Indigo told Genesis that he has a college degree in business and can take care of them and that he wanted her to be his wife. Then Genesis mentioned to Indigo trouble usually followed her where ever she goes and she was constantly hounded and questioned by people. Indigo became Genesis hero and refused to listen to negative and insulting rumors about her relinquishing solemn secrecy of her privacy and he loved her dearly. Well, the inseparable duet had a private marriage ceremony and they drove to a cottage far away from the city. After arriving to the lodge within their intimate solitude of privacy Indigo's hormones accelerated when he carried Genesis into the cabin. After exposing their nakedness Indigo romanced every part of Genesis uncovered body with intense passion which overtook her craving for true love. Altogether, late during the eve of night Indigo and Genesis love making climaxed into a bursting echo of splendor as they adored each other's intimacy. Then under the bright and shimmering moonlight to the doorway of romance which they could see the family tree (third eye) and conceived a primordial egg. However, Indigo was attracted to Genesis beautiful brown frame and he continued to made love to every inch of her body expressing creativity of intense emotion. Afterwards, Indigo surprises Genesis with news that they're were going on a honeymoon cruise across the Mediterranean Sea throughout the terrain. After the two boarded the cruise ship it was a relaxing and navigating adventure while they enjoyed appetizers and savory cuisine during the voyage to the cradle of civilization. While Indigo sipped on imported wine and drinks containing liquor flavored cocktails enhanced his observation of the peninsula during sailing on the gigantic transport which was much needed adventure for Genesis. As the two kindred spirits glimpsed at the beautiful turquoise blue ocean of waves overlooking ancient historical cities of Algiers, Jerusalem, Barcelona and they noticed fisherman pulling in fresh fish in from the villages. When the cruise line and cargo pulled in into the port the happy couple went on a tour of a natural vegetation. The tour consisted of evergreen, oak, cypress and sycamore, tropical fruit, olive, fig, citrus and walnut trees. Grape vineyards were plentiful and fresh herbs of lavender, rosemary, thyme and sage scented the regions atmosphere. After checking into a choice hotel Indigo and Genesis went on a sightseeing odyssey through long extended highways surrounding the Libyan Sea just north of the African coast. The ancient region interested the two lovers as they glimpsed at popular interior decorating concepts that was phenomenal masterpieces. Whereas, attributing the exhibition of rusty burnt colors laying yellow and orange stain which was important to consider for dark cabinetry, iron wall decor and furniture. Kitchens were sculptured of decorated baskets and copper accessories, textures contrasted metal wall tapestry colors of cinnamon, olive and gold for decorating themes. Indigo and Genesis navigated throughout the Alboran Sea west part of the Mediterranean. Then north of Spain, Morocco and south of Algeria observatory where they encountered Egypt's ancient civilization statues of pharaohs (hem-ek) who ruled. The long tour of the Nile river (Hapi) known as the father of the African peninsula and the longest in the world. Rising south of the equator and flowing to northeast Africa into the Mediterranean Sea stretching throughout the Nile river nearly 4,132 miles with the basin including a part of the Congo, Kenya, the Sudan, Tanzania, Burundi, Ethiopia, Egypt and Uganda. The river is black in color and sediment material is carried by flooding and the mud is so dark that it gave the land the original name Kemet meaning black. It was an unforgettable trip for the two and after returning to the states they relocated and embarked on a new horizon. The countryside of New Jersey where Genesis was more comfortable with people and her surroundings. The two moved onto a cabin encircled by a captivating forest that had a wine cellar filled with fine wine fermented from grapes. The cottage was within a mile radius of the Atlantic Ocean then Indigo and Genesis bought several acers of the land. A long stretch of properties across from the beach where apartments combine with units for occupying businesses which housed their people. It was for to give them a fair price of common wealth and Genesis could sell her line of retail. Some of the units that Indigo and Genesis built were for extended night stays for visitors which serviced a full kitchen. Other units were structured for large gatherings and entertainment including a jazz and blues club with a full kitchen to service guest featuring a pioneer of artist from around the world. Emphasizing musicians who were associated with instruments including: Saxophone, trumpet, double bass, clarinet, drums, piano, trombone, cornet, acoustic guitar, telecaster and sometimes a harp or harmonica ensemble. There was a second level to accommodate any size function and the walls were consolidated of photos of historical greats and African American Art. The club also, were composed of hip hop, poetry readings, stand-up comedy and plays for entertainment featuring talent from everywhere and some who were hoping for exposure. Long streets were combine of vendors displaying their talent or creativity and sold merchandise by the call of African drummers. Real estate took off quickly and there were plenty of investors one who occupied an African supermarket selling organic food. Another opened a Sankofa cafe' meaning to return celebrating the spirit of the ancestors, planning events featuring fire shows, music theatre and slide presentations of the abuse on slave ships coming over and the project was a huge success.

Genesis the Cosmic Goddess
Chapter 11

Genesis told Indigo that she was born with a veil over her face which blessed her with extrasensory perception (ESP) and when concentrating hard enough she can activate energy. Indigo responded wow! You were acknowledged by your ancestors Genesis and that is such a great honor but, I knew there was something special about you. However, with the veil you can see beyond the deception and without it your exposed to a false world. Then actually you are a chosen High Priestess and the vessel of the unconscious mind is to ready the children of God for the transition into the next life but, they didn't recognize you. Therefore, many desperately work for the beast who helped turned the aboriginal family into ungodly beings that is not capable of doing what is right just to receive a pay check. Yes, Genesis responded then she finally told Indigo about her mother's hatred towards her and he insisted on complete separation for the unforgivable actions. Now Genesis can focus on the prophecy of her veil so, she ate healthy and wholesome fresh meals. Through an intake of alkaline water, fresh fruits, vegetables, herbs, barks and roots that her body needed to maintain good health and Genesis rested from the stress of hardships. Then Genesis got rid of the mechanical devices such as her cell phone, computer, T.V., appliances that released radiation blocking her ability to tap into her divine power. She fasted and meditated daily so, she could hear the call from the ancestor's praying to give thanks in the morning, noon and evening. Genesis often called upon her kinsmen the Orishas who represent sacred knowledge, making up seven African powers. Elegua, the first deity who open the path to mankind, ruling the crossroads traveled in matters of destiny and fate through meditation before reaching other Orishas. Then Yemaya the Yoruba deity of motherhood and queen of the sea solving matters of fertility and spiritual growth also, she is the source of strength in times of emotional crisis. Oshun, the goddess guiding in love, desire and abundance who support those in growth and transition. Chango the god of lighting, power, sensuality and passion together with Oshun, Yemaya, Obatala representing the four pillars of the Orishas and he is the beacon of strength and dignity. Obatala the eldest admired creator of mankind, calling on in matters of legal issues and known to be fair to the innocent in judgement. Oya, the deity carrying fierce energy and the communicator between the living and the dead. A warrior female who can summons tornados, use lighting to battle against enemies and a favored lover of Chango. Ogun, the protective father figure deity that enjoys the wilderness and one who help to strengthen for a battle against enemies. Together these seven deities represent a force of guidance and strength through life tribulations. Meanwhile, after Genesis acknowledged what she was told by the African shaman that births, solutions and expirations date was already written on the walls of Kemet temples in the motherland. One bright summer day when Genesis was in private she was meditating and begin to astral travel which took her to destinations in her immediate future. There she experienced herself training in Tai Chi Bo that is affiliated with healing internal power, soul regeneration and determination. Abiding by the attributions of the goddess Maat and cleansing with salts from the dead sea which connects to the Atlantic Ocean, Europe, west to Asia, north Africa nearly surrounded by land. Genesis transformed into a supreme goddess that her ancestors planned surrendering her to the promise freedom. Shortly, the planet began to shower with ravishing rains causing Genesis to pretentiously undergo wisdom. Overall, she was stronger mentally, physical and emotionally prepared for an introduction with the descendants. Meanwhile, on another day after returning from astral traveling Genesis experimented with a combination of delightful sounds, rhythms, colors, tasting, touching and smelling as she understood it to rejuvenate her functional components. Suddenly, the circuits in her third eye opened giving her extra sharp vision, stronger insight, psychic ability, telekinesis and memory power during an accelerated discharge of carbon. Then cumulative clouds begin developing into a fierce storm rearranging the architectural structure on the earth and the foundation appeared different. Collectively, Genesis extracted water from the well at the cabin and burned candles for light during the night as she watched neighbors franticly pray for forgiveness thinking the world was ending. Immediately, after an outburst of the Sun (Ra) infused a current of enormous energy out of the heavens. The explosion raised the temperature to demolish the thermometer during a massive heatwave causing it to become hotter and hotter. Unexpectedly, the Sun out burst into solar flares creating a huge wave of over absorption of energy into Genesis body transforming her into a carbonated goddess. Then Genesis became ageless and her locked hair induced of wool electrified into a current of enormous power. The energy created a destructive affect and her molecules radiated into an emerging force reproducing Genesis body into a protective shield of armor. During an intense routine of training the change was new so, she spent a lot of time experimenting using her locked hair as a weapon. While Genesis focused on moving and slamming heavy objects with her hair out of amazement she examined herself as she mastered the art of the newfound transition. After successfully sharping her skills for the day of retribution Genesis fashion a warrior costume made of pure gold. Accessing the garment with topaz to physical heal her body, amethyst representing spirituality and quartz representing clarity then added precious metals which accompanied a snake head band. The crown represented rebirth or protecting the harvest of ancient deities who created the cosmic egg and Genesis wore a gold arm, wrist and ankle strap. Meanwhile, Genesis garnished her face with African war paint which complimented a soft comfortable leather platform sandal. Now, the season has arrived for Genesis to meet her descendants in paradise and she then receives a call from them without any manufactured instruments. After Genesis incurred a telepathic ability she communicated with them during an announcement of her acclaim. Then Genesis ascended out of the African root of the tree of life and disbursed into a constellation of stars and orbited throughout the galaxy. Genesis didn't have protective gear because carbon adjusted her physical activity in the cosmic zone of all living matter. 9 Ether which is a combination of gases existing in nature which maximized into the highest power in the universe. Appointing Genesis above the 6 Ether gene that is scientifically distant from solar activity and delinquent of favor within alien encounter. Throughout, Genesis navigation in the cosmos she didn't need fuel or an engine that operate on low altitude or can experience a software shutdown. Maybe even burst into flames, Genesis gravitational current pulled her naturally an at tremendous speed startling the test results into reality. Now, the cosmos was based on a foundation of social functions embracing peaceful and happy relationships within the family tree. The concept was Instilled by ancestor Maat and her 48 attributions to restore peace in the dominion. Maat was one of the earlier Neter's who taught divine principles of the truth influencing the Five pointed star (Seba) and controlling the seasons. However, the timeline was approaching the coming age and Genesis was honored with the ankh that she attached to her garment the key to eternal life. Welcoming Genesis into the ancient family and the promised utopia as she witnessed many beautiful civilizations in the heavens. After Genesis witnessed other planets in the solar system which were civilized with people resembling herself then she saw the same monuments that were established on earth such as the Pyramids, Sphinx, and Obelisk. Afterwards, Genesis was acquainted with Asuar, Aset and Heru the ancient African deities who has the authority of hierarchy to rule heaven and earth. Then the descendants took Genesis on a tour of the cosmos and in view of the Sun it was larger there and never set on certain planets without the moon in honor of Ra who give life force energy. Genesis finally met the educator of languages named Mdw ra n kmt meaning the spoken word in the temple who teaches many African languages. A Kemet favorite the Mdw Ntcher was the oldest known Afo-asiatic language of the family tree. Dated nearly 2690 BC making it one of the oldest recorded languages known equivalent to the Sumerians associated with coffin and pyramid text. The coffin text emphasized accessing into the afterlife where souls can transition into a successful passage across Tuat (the land of the dead) a road that must be traveled to receive salvation. Then the pyramid text which were carved on the walls in the chambers and corridors during the 5th and 6th dynasties of the Kemet kingdom.

Hieroglyphic inscription was a primary concern to protect the patriarchs remains after death to assist in ascending into the heaven's. Next Genesis was taught the Amharic language the official Semitic tongue of Ethiopia an estimated population of 85 million people. Swahili also, is a common language of the Bantu people that is widespread in Africa but, was changed by the Arabs for easier understanding. Sawhili being the mother tongue of the people who inhabit 1500 km stretch of the east coast territory from southern Somalia to northern Mozambique. The forth language Genesis learned was Twi a dialect of Akan where nearly 7 million Twi speakers use which is widely spread in Ghana, west Africa and they could speak many other languages. During Genesis dwelling into the heavenly abode she was amazed to such incredible sights, sounds welcomed by drums and bells which fill her with harmony. Also, appeared aromas of fresh grown herbs and flowers which rejuvenated the atmosphere while she delighted herself in the traditional practices. Genesis noticed that the star was over flowing with milk and honey in an abundance of pure springs of water. Other civilizations were splendidly decorated in fine jewels, silver, gold, precious stones, crystals, platinum, copper and valuable minerals they mined for and these resources was backed in the equivalent of trillions. Everyone was growing their own gardens filled with fresh herbs, flowers and vegetables were common on the planet. Genesis ancestor's demeanor was courteous and their appearance was inherent while their essence was magnified by the sweet caressing Sun. Their voice was like the sound of vibrating instruments connecting with their luminary bodies consolidating light of their eternal existence. Genesis collaborated with the body of configurational planets which revolved around the sun and moon that followed her everywhere rejoicing and obeying her every command. The clothing her ancestors wore was consciously designed linen, accentuating the body of the wearer for an attractive appeal. Jewelry was fashioned of precious metals, stones, cowrie shells, beads, jewels and crystals with healing properties representing spirituality from the fertile sphere. Equipment wasn't needed to plow the fruitful civilization they just threw down seeds that multiplied a harvest and in abundance. At times when Genesis traveled about the solar system she encountered her neighbor the moon star. A cosmic body of women who welcomed Genesis by a feast discussing the structure of the eon's cycle when planets occupy the same process. However, Genesis received a residency in the peaceful lodging that was enhanced by total happiness within a realm of female energy. The ancient women possess powerful attributes and are masters of occult knowledge, wisdom and etiquette so, they continued to council Genesis along with the elders. They were experts in science, alchemy, astronomy, agriculture and architecture, hunting, and warfare to add to Genesis momentum for a battle of non-negotiating interest. The Instructors coached Genesis in completing the training course starting with her telekinesis power influenced by manipulating objects with the force of the mind. Then a common method for healing the sick was to apply warm hands on the individual allowing balancing forces of the universe to manifest was a major part of the educational routine. Genesis was taught many healing methods but her favorite procedure was carved out of the pyramids of higher consciousness. Using heat to flow into humongous energy through compounds causing the body and mind to heal itself. The next power Genesis possessed was telepathic a capability using the mind to send data to communicate by transporting energy within the vehicle from one person to another. Genesis received keen eyesight which was sharp as a bird that soars at high altitude spotting objects from miles away reaching within hundreds of feet. Seeing sights beyond 20/20 vision 4 to 8 times keener than humans who have perfect vision on the planet. Although, Genesis amplified outstanding physical strength and could lift enormous pieces of solid iron and steel within her beautiful built frame was an outstanding enactment. Then Genesis ability to fly was activated by a gravitational force pulling her solar disc (Heru Behudet) on a strong iron alloy material that controlled her movement from one place to another by cosmic activity from outer space. After the process of renewal Genesis returned to earth as a reincarnated figure rebelling against falling back to a lower dimension but, bringing the concept of divinity and superiority into a blessed reality. Genesis landed on African soil near the Giza Plato where she entered the three pyramids below the threshold of Orion's belt and Sirius. When the king chamber open's Genesis witnessed the presence of the ancient deity Ausar (Ra Un Nefer Amen) readying for judgement. A person name Paut Neter means "The story of you and me" was waiting to guide Genesis throughout the boundaries within. There she noticed that walls are made of crystal granite the antenna used for ascending and descending contacts to the heavens and earth. There was no trace of a lineage in the study of anyone in the bible but, everyone governed land for themselves under the goddess Maat principles. Next Genesis returned to America on her flying wing disk (Heru Behudet) which navigated by gravity pulling her naturally. When she arrived to the fifty states a massive heatwave fiercely opened causing it to become hotter and hotter sending the temperature to accelerate demolishing the thermometer. The intense glow the Sun (Ra) continued to reinforce Genesis energy grid distributing a network of amazing power absorbing into her circuits. Meanwhile, negotiating interest wasn't considered within the independent monarchy to restore peace but, to free brothers and sisters who were taken captive. The sons and daughters of the universal creator was to return Africa where they belong in the homeland until further notice of change in the states. Meanwhile, Genesis people who were still struggling from the aftermath of slavery throwing their pearls before swine (enemy). Integrating and mix-breeding accelerated with a species who DNA make-up is different causing a change of African American's well-proportioned body structure. The indigenous people were so, caught up to integrate with Lucifer not realizing that they were falling from the 3nd dimension into a 2nd dimension. Whereas, their souls would be lost forever not having the opportunity for redemption and embrace the return of the traditional African Kabbalah. Chiefly, Genesis then composed and organized a resistance army of warriors for a stand-by siege who were brothers and sisters born with a veil over their face that she encountered as a traveling salesperson. Genesis then influenced her soldiers to await her command in a battle for freedom. Then amongst them she selected high ranking fighters to set up a system of annihilation against the evil empire. Recruiting five brothers and seven sisters, two of them Orisha kinsmen totaling twelve carefully chosen entourage and Genesis was thirteen. Although, the selection was difficult because these Deities appearance was identical and they could possibly betray the mission. There is Isis the goddess of wisdom, protection, fertility and magic (super natural). Nephthys (Nebet Het) Isis twin sister goddess of the underworld, intuition and initiation of mysteries and the chalice is her symbol and javelin is her most use weapon. The Yoruba Goddess Oya the warrior who summons tornadoes and lighting to battle against an enemy favorite weapon of war is the spear. Then Ogun the Orisha an outdoorsman who bring strength and protection to fight in battle, weapon of war is the club. Amun Ra the Sun god who created civilization and an afterlife, skilled at using every weapon. Heru Behudet one who is royal and infamous for his soaring winged disc who is considered amusing by teasing elders demonstrating his special effects. Maat representing a fixed point of light which influence's life and one who control the seasons and master the whip. Apis a manifestation of Path another god of creation and the weapon of chose was knife throwing. Venus, the goddess second from the Sun absorbing rays specializing in using the bow and arrow. Tehuti representing the staff of the moon god influencing writing, wisdom and his favorite weapon is the spear. Then Sekhmet goddess of avenging force and justice skilled at using all weapons but, the most used is the sword. Wadjet the cobra goddess of lower Kemet representing the "fiery eye of Re" when two Urareus symbols is seen on the side of the wing disk which means to spit fire at an approaching enemy and chosen weapon is the spear. Ra (Re) God of overcoming enemies, life force energy, vitality and symbol is the sun disk and weapon preferred is the axe. Together they all master several deadly weapons skillfully including the bow and arrow, axe, sword, club, whip, javelin, hatchet, spear and so, forth then these thirteen warriors have amazing combat techniques. These amazing hero's (Heru) trained various wild and exotic animals including: lions, leopards, gorilla's, elephants, bulls and so forth in an invasion. The fearless warriors were anxious to war against the earthlings so, they painted their face with African war paint and dressed themselves in warrior fighting gear. Genesis then organized her assisting army of soldiers who were on a stand-by awaiting her command to annihilate the evil empire that portrayed an image of greed and corruption. Then informed her crew that if anyone abuse their power a penalty will be incurred through hard punishment. Since Genesis was the highest ranking general and expert fighter who taught her warriors many skills that she learned during her training in resistance of the enemy. Afterwards, Genesis flew on her winged disk taking along the twelve warriors each one operating their own navigation system to greet the eternal family. After arriving the ancestors embraced them and opened the gateway of energy from the Sun to fully flow into their bodies and long locked hair (9 ether). Earth was impossible to charge an abundance of power because of chemicals and radiation that slow down the gravitational movement and energy process. Therefore, in the star gate the warrior's bodies infused more carbonized compounds which intensified force for emerging against an enemy of warfare. Once the session ended then the established plan of retribution by the cosmic gods ordered and charged Genesis to stop the suffering of her people. However, the royal kingdom proclaimed a declaration on the throne that it was time to launch war because the children of the all mighty creator had not received reparations. The system refused to issue any tender for the loss, misfortune or set up a reunion with African descendants to prove that they have a capacity for love. Considering that the aboriginal people heritage isn't based on European names and way of living but, it characterized failure by omitting change for better. The rulers on earth wanted the public to think that everything was normal and the administration was giving a long time to replace all the wealth that they had robed from the children of the God. In regards to African Americans rights to return to their former way of life but, they chose to continue to enslave themselves by honoring a racist confederacy. Then white supremacist began instigating in arrogance and a mind-set in southern regions in a sophisticated manner Jim crow anti-black laws insisting that all men aren't equal. However, in many parts of the deep south in the 21st century the spirit of Jim Crow laws was still live which is not a place for black people to put up with. Therefore, Genesis ancestors advised her to intelligently form a committee where no ruler would again comply with foreign demands against her people in an act of corruption. Afterwards, the elders demanded that it was time to destroy the evil empire and finalized the committee meeting for starting the siege to free her people. Once the meeting ended Genesis orbited back to the U.S.A. soaring like a falcon with Sashet the goddess of writing to record and report the events. Meanwhile, one bright sunny day Genesis met up with her best friend Dawn and was chilling in a nearby a popular west Indian restaurant. The restaurant played live reggae chilling over vegetarian cuisine that was filled with fresh amaranth (callaloo) and plantain with a Ting beverage. Genesis was wearing comfortable linen accenting precious stones, crystals, with cowrie shells to compliment her clothing, hair and sandals. Dawn wore a European outfit which had some imaginary appeal but, didn't bring out her true beauty. The two haven't seen in each other in a long time and while catching up on old times Dawn noticed a change in Genesis. Just when Genesis told Dawn that she has a husband and they own property in Africa Dawn ask Genesis why make such a tremendous move. Genesis responded in the states riches can be achieved for those who are in business for themselves. Although, America has power and an image to up-hold but, it's over run by foreigners who are reaping the benefits. Dawn, I was tired of being constantly robed of everything I worked hard for, robed of my family as you know, robed of education, robed by the police. Lied to by doctors and lawyers who seldom tell the truth and witnessing brothers and sisters get incarcerated for trying to escape the hell brought on by a divided and unjust country when each race live with they're own kind. Tired of watching my people sell their souls for sex and money just to appear as an integrated nigger and are considered second class citizen's. I am tired of fighting against the beast which is obvious a hopeless cause. Dawn responded, I know that's right and Genesis continued to say that people of color are righteous by nature and lived free in the homeland which is abundant in resources until Lucifer came along. Then one day the salvage beast who were strange and different enslaved and dehumanized the Africans committing the greatest sin known to man. People of African descent can be peaceful but, perform poorly when surrounded and corrupted then influenced by other groups. Suddenly, a bad storm brew bringing heavy rainfall, hail and strong winds knocking down enormous size trees and turning over heavy objects. Dawn noticed a change in Genesis that something was different about her asking what's going on. Unexpectedly, citizens began to scream in panic about a family being trapped under debris then Genesis and Dawn rushed to the assiduous scene. Immediately, Genesis observed an automobile crash where a Caucasian family was trapped beneath heavy trees and branches that nearly crushed them to death. Then an adrenaline release occurred in Genesis response to the danger as an entangled family faced the crisis and she pulled the door off the hinge that was jammed. Remarkably, Genesis magnetic locks grabbed, lifted and placed the family on the sidewalk for safety. A young male boy was badly hurt sustaining a head trauma and Genesis healed his bloody wounds by touching the bodily damage that penetrated from her hands. Allowing heat to flow from universal organisms to heal the painful condition then Dawn and the public was amazed by Genesis astonishing abilities. News Reporters quickly entered the scene and were photographing and recording footage of the shocking event questioning Genesis about her super natural power, status and homage. Dawn was impressed by Genesis phenomenal strength demonstrated and was waiting to confront her concerning the incident but, miraculously she disappeared. The event hit the front page of every daily newspaper across the country which got the attention of a local entertainment promoter name Joe who noticed the article. Joe was hoping to boost business so, he sent Genesis an invitation challenging her to a duel against four of the nation greatest female champions. Introducing: beast a Caucasian fighter, Pitbull a sister, Crusher a sister and Assassin an Asian. Genesis met and accepted the promotors terms and the proceeds will go towards educating orphans. Then Joe instructed her that the competition will consist of mostly wrestling, boxing and martial arts. Prior to the fight in a conference Genesis was introduced with a publicize interview of the professional fighters and their rank. A heavy weight division of women fighters who punch the hardest, endure the most pain and score the most knockouts, most slams, known for giving black eyes, bloody noses and busted testicles. These champions were vicious and known to break bones and extremely dangerous putting Genesis at her own risk. The fight will take place at the Grand garden arena located at 5 Penn Plaza, 1001 in N.Y.C. at 7th Ave.

between 31st and 33rd street and the fight will be the U.S. Vs. Africa. Meanwhile, Genesis entourage Dawn, Jade and Deka showed up for the fight and inside of the arena they were sitting in the audience waiting to support her. At the event Dawn told Jade and Deka about Genesis miraculous ability when focusing she can activate enormous and magical power and they responded wow! that's incredible. Genesis loved Indigo so, she told him about the match which was against four professional fighters and in shock Indigo goes with her to the stadium. After arriving they noticed Genesis friends Dawn, Jade, and Deka sitting in the audience waiting to support her. Indigo trusted Genesis when she informed him about her ESP but, he commented on how dangerous the opponents looked and blood thirsty with a look of concern. Genesis face was garnished with African war paint and she was bare footed wearing a warrior costume. The costume accented a gold arm, wrist and ankle band engraved of topaz to heal any sustained injury, amethyst and quartz. Genesis kissed Indigo on the cheek saying it will be alright and approached the ring as the crowd cheered in favor of the assailants. Before the fight started Genesis looked at Indigo and face the first opponent known for her hard hits as the referee rings the bell. Beast is showing off her muscular physique who is known for breaking chains and bars. Then rushes Genesis with a powerful blow to the abdomen but Genesis armor affect from the magnetic grid safeguarded her and the blow was barely felt. Beast begin throwing Genesis into the ropes attempting to smash her but, she maneuvered out of the way and grabs Beast neck in a strong hold. The other trio of fighters are studying Genesis defense strategy as Beast was excited when Genesis stumbled and fell due to a slip and fall from her opponent (Beast laughs crazed). The crowd cheers for blood as Genesis gets up slinging her magnetic long lock hair around Beast neck and slams her across the platform. Then Beast rumbled into the audience unconscious and is escorted out of the arena and Indigo, Dawn, Jade and Deka amazed, applauding and cheering loudly. The bell rings and the second champion undefeated fighter Crusher who is 7 feet tall with 20 inch biceps approaches the ring known for her enormous physical strength lifting over 200 pounds. Crusher body slammed Genesis on the canvas dropping her solid weight on Genesis causing her to struggle to get up. Then Crusher advances quickly towards the opponent and the adversary gives Genesis an unexpected kick to her abdomen while she wasn't focusing. The hit caused Genesis to stumble but, Crusher hurt her foot on the hard surface of Genesis armored body. Crusher then lifted Genesis over her head spinning her around and tossed her with a mighty force dropping her on the canvas. Genesis stumbles to get up and is thrown into the rope liner by Crushers mighty force and got caught into a twist in the ring. Indigo, Dawn, Jade and Deka look on with worry as the crowd cheers in Crushers favor. Then Genesis manage to break out of the twist in the ring using her magnetic long locks to strike a hard blow like the sting of a serpent knocking Crusher out. One, two, three counts by the referee Crusher is out and the crowd chants as Crusher is being carried out (the audience think the match is funny). The third champion fighter is Pitbull known for locking in on the opponent with her teeth and ripping off the flesh. The bell rings and Pitbull laughs deranged as she moves in on Genesis putting her in a bear hug with the intentions to cause her organs to explode. As adrenaline rushes through Genesis circuits she breaks loose from the hold of the attack by Pitbull using the magnetic charge of currents from her locked hair.

Zapping Pitbull with a fatal shocking force of powerful energy leaving her body in a shaking temporary collapse onto the platform. After Pitbull struggle to get up she pause in shock before slowly moving in on Genesis heading towards her attempting to rip the flesh with her teeth. Pitbull miss but, instead gives Genesis a hard body slam then jump up and down as if she is defeated. Genesis then toil to get up and she grabs Pitbull by the arm slinging her around in circles releasing her to fall firmly on her face bursting her nose into a bleed and Pitbull is taken out shameful. The last champion fighter is Assassin famous for her most devastating knockouts and catching cannon balls at close range. The referee rings the bell Assassin grabs and lift Genesis up on her shoulders and spun her around the platform dropping her neck on the rope causing a chocking affect. In revenge Genesis use her telekinesis power and flip the giant Assassin over and over up into the air pounding her into the canvas and she slowly gets up. Assassin is afraid of Genesis but, she doesn't want her to know it rushing Genesis by bouncing off the rope attempting to grab her but, throw a kick to Genesis. Genesis try to block the hits with her hands as they battle hard with continued blows causing Genesis to bleed while the topaz crystal is healing the wound then Assassin thinks she got the best of her. Genesis then uses her telekinesis power to manipulate energy causing Assassin to flip up into the air and fall to the platform breaking her legs. The bell rings and the referee lifts Genesis arms as the winner (the crowd is shouting) in favor of Genesis then Indigo and her friends Dawn, Jade and Deka approaches to embrace her. While a surrounding mob of citizens who are amazed by Genesis exceptional abilities rushes to applaud her then she goes to her residence to rest. The next day after the fight was over Genesis continued selling ethnic products as if nothing had happened even though her ancestors blessed her with an enormous amount of treasure. Meanwhile, to keep up with how Genesis people were progressing sadly they were still divided hating one another and struggling to pay bills. Later, the aboriginal people started to get fed-up with the oppression and begin to rebellion after communicating with each other demanding that the administration offer them better. After coming into consciousness through a network of information the children of antiquity didn't appreciate being lied to for the gain of prosperity. However, that evening while Genesis watched the news and saw black people rioting in different parts of the nation expressing their feelings of loss. Brothers and sisters wanted out of the cage so, they destroyed much of America's property causing the police to get involved which brought about martial law. Genesis continued to watch the program observing the up-roar of her people who started pushing for self-determination. Genesis begin to feel that there was some hope after all and she knew that the decision they made would not be an easy one for those who were comfortable. Now, the time has come when Genesis broaden her focus for an initiated plan ordered by the cosmic gods who asked her if there are souls worth saving. After answering the deities through a telepathic method responding there may be a few. After the goddess Seshat the recorder of the children of the gods gave Genesis a census stating that she was still searching for righteous souls. Afterwards, Genesis is becoming weak due to the extreme measure of chemicals and radiation on the planet within a large perimeter of the poison. Therefore, she and Seshat temporarily flew on their wing disk pulled a by gravitational current to the cosmos for rejuvenation and shortly returned. After meeting with the heavenly host

Genesis and Seshat look at each other explaining that there is mutiny on earth and our people are up-rooted. However, the prophecy of grandma, the female shaman and the revelation giving to Genesis by an ancestor in a conversation unfolded. Now, the country was falling apart economically as the job market slowly disappeared and chaos impacted the commonwealth. Many people were dying and became sick from a distribution of radioactive food and water which depopulated masses of people. Although, America was struck by enormous earthquakes in various places particularly in New York. The sun (ra) inside of the asteroid belt exploded and the heat index rose astronomically high changing the civilization land mass. The event ended the food supply and people was disorderly looting to find whatever surplus that might be available. Many citizens went underground particularly people who were pigment deficient hiding themselves from the sun and those who stay above ground were covering the windows with panels. Then people of color who were ignorant about carbon and followed the recessive gene people below the surface because they were not educated on embracing the blessing of Ra. These were the aboriginal ones who went against the plan of god honoring Lucifer and will be with them trapped in an underground feud with no way out. Suddenly, noticing that they're skin turned pale (Seth) because they lost the righteous path and were no longer the pro-type of the all mighty god. Then the resources under the ground ran out so, those who survived had to rely on cannibalism to survive. Meanwhile, people on top of the ground was trying to find an escape while others were left behind and became vicious towards one another in an explosive manner. Although America was never meant for African Americans to stay but, to flee from the salvage beast who run the country. Whereas, safety concerns were at an astronomical high while children became a danger to society and were ungrateful to their parents. Computers crashed due to an overload of running on the power grid causing a shutdown where people had to rely on living off the land. However, the ancestors ordered an evacuation of the anointed ones before the great battle to take back the earth for spiritual living. All hell broke loose and those who were left behind ended up in camps and exterminated after refusing to comply with a mandatory vaccine order. A trumpet sounded in the cosmos alerting soldiers to stay on stand-by for an indisputable war while they awaited Genesis command. Genesis was blessed from her ancestors in a currency of gold, silver and jewels from natural resources in the equivalent of trillions. Therefore, Genesis knew that America was corrupt and driven by greed so, she attempted to negotiate a financial agreement for the freedom for others and failed. After compromising was neglected Genesis was fed up with the dominating empire so, the descendants ordered her to combat against the earthly beings. Starting with New York city Genesis went about using every capability that she bestowed to destroy the root of the problem. Awakening the country in extreme anxiety while flying in on her large space craft that hovered in the air maneuvering through the clouds. Then landing on the surface of earth hiding in the forest by an invisible current out of the cosmos. Genesis used her telekinesis ability for slamming large stones, iron and steel through the windows of homes and businesses, spotting objects from miles away with her keen eye sight. Snatching hostages from their homes and businesses taking them to planet void which lack resources until they're death. Now, the U.S. government was ferocious ordering every war tank, jet, missile, bombs and firearms available in a counter attack creating a star and ground war. Although, Genesis could maneuver by the speed of light while hiding in the clouds which made it difficult for American fighter jets to catch and conquer her. Genesis was about to send for her warriors then a pilot mentioned to his co-pilot dawn, how are we going to catch and destroy her. Substantially, the American military struggled to operate jets flying slow on fuel with obsolete equipment compared to gravitational pull by their opponent. A force field surrounded and protected Genesis as she got revenge on the enemy while snatching propelled airplanes out of the sky using her telekinesis capability. Citizens looked on in shock witnessing that the American war machine was not affective enough to withstand the goddess. Flying capsules that was on stand-by took off headed for outer space to escape the chaos but, got caught in a magnetic current and the software malfunction causing the crafts to explode. Missiles were ordered and fired towards the goddess on her starship but, ejected off an energy shield. The U.S. military was cocky and bullied countries globally using software but, realized that they were no match for Genesis. On the ground troops were ordered to take out Genesis with the weapons that they thought were sophisticated but, was embarrassing out of date. Genesis used her locked hair to slash the flesh off the skin of the American soldiers and one attempted to run away and she rip off his clothing leaving him running away naked. Meanwhile, the technology on Genesis large space craft was advanced and protected by the magnetic shield causing firearms to bounce off. However, more of Genesis people were pulled by the gravitational current along with other groups and put into her space craft then dropped off on planet void which lack resources and they could cause no more enslavement and harm to citizens. The military failed miserably ending in an unsettled catastrophe admitting that nothing is more powerful than nature and that the universe belonged to god. Afterwards, America lost their power and was overthrown and the stars began to fall out of the sky renewing the wretched earth cleansing the former frontier creating a new civilization. Then dark matter accelerated and consumed the planet developing rapidly within over one billion galaxies in the universe. The darkness transformed into an existence which had reached a limit beyond itself causing color deficiency to lack completeness. It awakened the children of God that was left behind as the people from another planet revived the lost remnants and they cried for joy. Then this left bunch begged to be accepted into the eternal home but, they were not commendable and was left wandering. Additionally, it became known that they were god children who worshiped a false god and a few turned pale (Seth) but, others would be transitioned back to planet earth for another chance to repent. Primarily, in the navigation of their egg which landed on earth (3D) until it formed into a loving being who will live with all mighty god. Other inhabitants barbarously sorted through left over salvage after the war while fighting lepers (zombies) who were afflicted by the scorching Sun (Ra). Hideous looking creatures yelling and screaming in pain in their state of existence as hemophiliacs walked about the nights awaiting to eat human flesh. Animals were an appetizing delight as the creatures returned to the valley of caves during sunrise to hide from blazing double digit temperatures. Meanwhile, after other the monsters went underground the golden age healed the land and those who had carbon were cured instantly causing them to become well mentally, physically and emotionally stronger. These children who were left behind discovered through information that they were the High Priest, liberators, Messiah's, Saviors all along that society was waiting on through DNA samples left in the hands of an African chemist who revealed the truth. Therefore, Massa had concealed this knowledge and made them ignorant, suspicious against their own people as the timeline expired to rule globally. Overall, the sons and daughters of the holy creator couldn't return to the family tree so, they were outraged. The sellout brothers and sisters who hid in secret hiding place with Caucasians at the end of the war is when house nigga's discovered that Massa had turned on them. Using food and hypodermic needles to inject poison into their bodies killing many after shutting off the power grid to steal their money. The brothers and sisters then destroyed recessive gene beings in a counter attack with knives, machete's and hatchet's in a bloody massacre because the deceiver didn't need them anymore. However, they killed their Caucasian wives, mix-breed children and then drank the poison destroying themselves because hope was gone after being tricked by the spell of kingu. Genesis noticed her family in the resistance that ended up joining the group who were killing the betrayer who deceived them in participating in ungodly actions and living against their own people. Afterwards, the children of antiquity realized that one can't serve mankind and love God neglecting their heritage which caused them to lose their soul.

Genesis inherit a kingdom in Africa the land of her origin
Chapter 12

Genesis didn't recognize many of the indigenous people because they had altered their appearance using methods that they adapted from the new world which caused attitudes and communication malfunctions. Therefore, her people appeared black but, they had become Europeanized and didn't embrace their roots anymore. However, Genesis family was left behind and she sobbed miserably knowing that her best friend Dawn's dilemma with worthless men caused her to lose her freedom because the concept in the family tree. The concept that many of her people had adapted to was forbidden in the new world where black matter replaced color deficiency. After the war ended Genesis envisioned a new America which formed a suitable structure of homes and businesses occupying lots of people. Meanwhile, a descendant from Egypt that Genesis didn't know heard of her fame and contacted her concerning ruling a kingdom that was to be replaced by a dying king. When Indigo and Genesis visited the kingdom it was beautiful and structured on a long royal cubit of land with lots of sectional properties within they will live. However, Genesis accepted the throne and took her wealth filled in hand crafted baskets fashioned of colorful beads and cowrie shells. Her riches over flowed with gold, silver, cooper coins and various types of jewels and migrated to Africa with finances in double digits of wealth combined in gifts they received during the term of their rule. Nearly two percent of Genesis people were convinced that they should crusade with the couple after suffering poor conditions in America. Overall, Indigo adored Genesis and spoiled her while they shared a monogamous relationship and his passion for her was deeply rooted that within a canopy of love they conceived another child and blessed with a boy and girl. Genesis named her daughter Sekhem meaning vital power and her son name was Mdw n Tr based on the written word after the ancient people of antiquity. Sekhem is a lot like her mother Genesis who instilled a demeanor of good in her and she is attractive with nice formed legs with a generous nature. Mdw n Tr grew up in the image of his father handsome and received a warrior spirit by hereditary. Indigo has a trustworthy soul, passionate, a sharp thinker and every woman's dream boat. Meanwhile, Genesis and Indigo philosophy of change was to please the population for better as life intended to be free, peaceful and righteous. Genesis and Indigo were a kindred pair who was moved by the spirit of love and family and would not accept an American concept of greed. Besides, in the new world there wasn't anything free in society it was structured for earning material wealth at the cost of others. However, chiefs who occupied African grasslands were familiar with the folklore about Genesis and loved the inseparable pair and they were blessed to inherit the palace to rule and reign. The palace was divided into sectional properties surrounded by palm trees, pyramids, an obelisk, a red, black and green flag hanging representing the land and the culture. The image that represented red was for protection of the region, black the color of the people and green for the land natural resources. King Indigo and his queen Genesis had seam tresses who custom made garments for the royal couple. The attire fashioned a soft comfortable linen garment, accenting a kufi crown designed of jewels and a soft leather sandal. Pure gold and a copper tone metals to accompany the snake headband in honor creation by the four powers (God) Ausar, Aset, Heru and Set. A Kemet ankh representing the key to eternal life, a collar jeweled necklace made in sequence of every birthstone. Pure gold wrist cuffs engraved in colorful crystals, bangles and a drinking solid gold goblet. Afterwards, Indigo changed his name to Amun-ra for commemorating African customs and as the king of gods to empower leadership by affirming a social standing with the kinsmen. Meanwhile, Amun-ra and queen Genesis formed a committee of twelve elders to organize and strategize concern's for the kingdom. The proclamation by order of the king was that that there will be no need for a census or a register of deeds. The King and Queen wanted the citizens to have ownership and a fair share of commonwealth and organized a council meeting to address the matter. There was was no need for public control so, the committee allowed patrons to determine their own fate. Whatever got out of control and the assembly of elders couldn't handle the incident then it would be settled before the majesty. Afterwards, the royal couple used their wealth to fashion the gigantic palace decorating the structure with fine jewels, gold, crystals, cooper and vibrant colors accompanying cathedral style decor. Then they hired professional interior designers to dress up each room which completed the kingdoms architectural blueprint. Nearly, exhausted the royal couple rested under the moonlight overlooking the ocean and sandy beach from the coastal breeze and palm trees relaxing on beds of bamboo frames. Arising early to greet Amen Ra then an ate a healthy alkaline cuisine with plenty of fruits and vegetables, nuts for energy and wellness. Diamonds was the essence of Genesis existence so, Amun ra loved his wife dearly and he ordered them to be a common decoration in the palace and throughout the land for memorable moments of their rule. The palace was overlooking a beautiful turquoise ocean view and the entire mass of land was abundantly appealing in the natural habitat accentuating lakes surrounding the Blue Nile. The territory complimented long cubits of roadways paved of emeralds, gold, jewels, crystals and the spirit of fire were used to light up communities at night, fluorescent lighting was forbidden. The animal kingdom was amazingly abundant running wild with no caged or bar environments for entertainment and charging fees. Amun-ra and Genesis dressed in fine linen just like the ancestors who endorsed special made copper tones, gold and beaded jewelry for their personal adornment and servants too. They owned a fleet of exquisite manually operated aircraft that navigated on an unseen gravitational movement. Every chauffeur was directed for courtesy and being friendly wearing expensive gold, beads and gemstone jewelry. There were many entrepreneurs and family owned businesses that operated restaurants, produced products, opened schools, theaters, herbal medical facilities, vineyards, clothing stores and sold fine jewelry amongst a few. They had it all and good health was a major concern of the king and queen and all food consumption acceded from healthy alkaline diets. Product manufacturing were produced by the abundance of natural resources abstracted out of the earth. Trees, bushes, shrubs, plants, pure water and so forth, was used for beauty and medical applications for the body. The indigenous people were not allowed to use harsh chemicals for cleaning or otherwise or it would deactivate their DNA robbing them of physical, mental and spiritual power. Every day on the bank of the sea shore which has an immaculate ocean scenery and beautiful palm trees that capture the essence of the atmosphere is where the royal family entertain locals and vacationers. Most local people were vegan but, guest was served from a buffet while local fishermen filleted and cooked fish caught fresh from the sea. Farmers brought in fresh fruits and vegetables straight from the garden while vendors sold merchandise, flowers and herbs enchanted the setting. Drummers were drumming, weavers were weaving, beading and potters were potting. There was singing, dancing, chanting and embracing one another with all day love, kindness and fun. Kings and queens and ordinary people came from all parts of the world just to make acquaintance in the royal kingdom. Rumors were spreading about the new leadership of Amun-Ra and Genesis in the land and many brothers and sisters were migrating from around the world for citizenship. The African kingdom was overwhelmed with request for residency and people were looking for freedom and a better way of life. Every corner of the palace stood warriors on each post to secure public safety. Drugs wasn't allowed in the kingdom because lives and communities were ruined due to the intake of the substance. However, if anyone was caught using or selling drugs in the palace or near the boundaries would sent into exile. Amun-ra and his queen demanded that there would be no pharmaceutical drugs for medicine, only herb, root and bark combinations they used for healing. Children went to school learning parenting skills, how to be husbands, wives and it was a mandatory part of the African curriculum. Pupils were taught to master the art of science, mathematics, geography, architecture, astronomy, languages, agriculture and medicine. Female students were taught the proper way to prepare and cook nutritional and balanced meals. Business and administration was also a part of the curriculum learning how to do business effectively, professionally and geography also, has it reward knowing where to travel and how. Yoga was a daily exercise routine in the class room with calming benefits and relaxing exercises to help transition students into everyday life. Allowing oneself to release tension also, focusing and maintaining posture by increasing flexibility on the body better while positioning movement. This method was commonly used in ancient African tradition for centering and clearing obstacles. Meditation was also another part of ancient practices for enriching daily life, healing and centering the body, mind and spirit. The concept was also, used to help manifest energy while focusing and exploring different ideas and learning how to connect with the divine creator. Chakras (Sefech Ba Ra) was introduced to children as another part of the culture because chakras are where energy flow into the body. Then channel and awake the body's controlling power giving one the ability to read aura's and activate tones and vibrations. Crown ruling higher knowledge, third eye ruling psychic skills and intuition, throat ruling communication, heart ruling love, energy ruling vital power, spleen ruling the sexual charka, sexual ruling passion, root ruling survival, hand ruling manual skills, foot ruling connection with the earth or independence. Reiki is one of Genesis favorite exercises because it is the gateway to destiny! (Home) as the reiki method is a sacred system of healing and expressing higher consciousness of people of African descent. The technique is based on an ancient healing system that uses energy to balance physical, mental and spiritual bodies. When powerful light forces along with the assistance of ancestors, spiritual guides and deities process it, is used for curing disease when energy comes from substances in the cosmos where gods and the goddesses live. This process is activated through meditation, giving thanks, tones, vibration, movement and other routines of spiritual work. The carbon curriculum is concerning a connecting relationship to the ancestors, spiritual guides and the creator who are the most spiritual inclined people in existence. However, Genesis suffering bought about a great change that bought her people back to their heritage which is what the students will pass on to their children. Young girls learned how to sew, spin thread, weave cloth and practiced home economics then boys learned fighting techniques and hunting skills. Collectively, to become warriors for protecting the village but, cooking meals was women's work and taboo for men which emphasized femininity (sissy). Whereas, in America it was a sick war amongst the sex's when homosexuals and lesbians took care of each other particularly men who neglected the woman. Precisely, in America boys rarely become men and many reach the age of maturity but, act like children. This concept doesn't exist in Africa it is forbidden to befriend or marry someone of that status. Every community and school had an alter or temple to give thanks to the holy creator for every earthly tiding and blessing received. In the heavens where the descendants live and on earth where they walk and talk in a daily routine didn't tolerate or benefit non-believers. No child past in school with failing grades and all disputes within the family had to go before the king and queen for solutions. Any man that would harm his wife or likewise physically, mentally or spiritually would be punished by imprisonment or a huge fine or penalized of marriage and maybe even exiled. It was against the law to throw down trash on the ground, pollute the lakes and oceans or even spit on the ground and old rusty or abandon items didn't exist. The kingdom demanded good habits and there was a dress code where no man, woman or child could expose themselves unless they were on the beach and they had to be discreet. There was no homelessness or hunger or mass production of food it was the responsibility of every family to maintain their own gardens and farm land. Everyone was encouraged to work independently for themselves or a start a family owned business and racism was not tolerated only equal or fair trade. There was no homosexuality, tattoos or sometimes there were light tribal art or face painting was popular but, slave wear was omitted. There was no need for lawyers and judges every concern was addressed before a council or Amun-ra and Genesis. There was a penalty for having sex outside of marriage in fear of spoiling the land and the concept of family with shame and the result was deportation. Wedding ceremonies were performed daily with African drums being the traditional choice of instrument for the celebration and announcement. These were the laws of the land and was enforced by the king and queen to keep order and balance in the kingdom.

THE END.

Authors page

I am a female of African descent who has a background in professional modeling and photography which was my earlier creative pursuits. I'm fun loving and enjoy sewing, crafting bead designs and get down with the simple things in life. The region of Africa and the magnificent glories and rich history will always be a major part of me. However, it was my pleasure and aspirations to bring about my own personal perspective on African culture and heritage of the black experience. Therefore, I hope that my accomplished work will inspire the indigenous people of becoming capable of one common interest. Obtaining knowledge of themselves by putting it into action, peace, love, wellness for the betterment of one another and the existence of man.

24470121R00093

Made in the USA
Columbia, SC
22 August 2018